WHO'S IN CONTROL?

DR. BALTER'S GUIDE TO DISCIPLINE
WITHOUT COMBAT

BY
DR. LAWRENCE BALTER

WITH
ANITA SHREVE

POSEIDON PRESS

NEW YORK LONDON TORONTO SYDNEY TOKYO

Poseidon Press
Simon & Schuster Building
Rockefeller Center
1230 Avenue of the Americas
New York, New York 10020

Designed by Irving Perkins Associates
Manufactured in the United States of America
1 3 5 7 9 10 8 6 4 2
3 5 7 9 10 8 6 4 2 *Pbk.*

Library of Congress Cataloging in Publication Data
Balter, Lawrence.
Who's in control?: Dr. Balter's guide to discipline without
combat/by Dr. Lawrence Balter with Anita Shreve.
p. cm.
Includes index.
1. Discipline of children. I. Shreve, Anita. II. Title.
HQ770.4.B35 1989
649'.64—dc19   *88-34145*
CIP
ISBN 0-671-62507-1
0-671-68227-X Pbk.

To Karen, again, and to my mother
—L. B.

To Douglas, Katherine, Charles and Emily
—A. S.

CONTENTS

FOREWORD

In my first book, *Dr. Balter's Child Sense*, I tried to help parents find practical solutions to the common problems of early childhood—from birth to five years of age. Underlying many of those common problems were conflicts between parent and child. Although I talked about discipline in that book—encouraging parents to look upon the goal of discipline as self-government for the child, and to avoid very harsh or punitive measures that might harm the child's self-esteem—I felt that the subject of discipline was of such magnitude, and of such concern to parents, that it warranted a closer look.

This book is that closer look. As in *Dr. Balter's Child Sense*, parents' concerns and questions have launched my discussions of discipline, which are both explanatory and practical in nature. In this book I am able to provide a more detailed examination of what continues to be one of the most important issues between a parent and a child. This book is also somewhat larger in scope, covering the years between infancy and the preteen stage of development. It is my hope that parents about to embark on child rearing, or parents currently concerned with these matters, will be able to use the two books together to form stronger, healthier and happier relationships with their children.

SPEAKING OF DISCIPLINE

On the radio, on television, in private practice and in my role as a professor of educational psychology, I am asked a great many child-rearing questions. The questions that are asked with the greatest frequency —and indeed, with the greatest urgency—are those that concern discipline.

Parents have always been worried about disciplining their children. Even in the more permissive era of the recent past, parents, for all their attempts to give their children freedom of expression and to foster individuality, still worried about whether or not they were spoiling their offspring. We all have an unpleasant mental image of a spoiled child—a child who seems not to respect adults or even other children, who appears to have uncontrollable impulses and little or no self-discipline and who lacks empathy for others.

As recently as two or three generations ago, the notion of sparing the rod and spoiling the child prevailed. Children were to be "trained," much as pets were, and if that training entailed regular beatings in order to control unruly tendencies, well, so be it. In some families, regular

13

beatings were meted out at the end of the day or the end of the week, not because any extraordinary behavior had occurred, but merely to keep the children in line. Not to dispense these regular punishments, it was thought, was to lose control of one's children.

As psychoanalysis grew in popularity, it led to a change in thinking about how to raise children. It became clearer that early childhood experiences played a significant and profound role in adult relationships. Therefore, a child's temperament, age, needs and development had to be considered in child rearing. Oppressing and suppressing a child's personality and desires were thought not to be in the best interests of the child. Child care and discipline became more child-centered.

Subsequently, these views occasionally were interpreted to mean that parents should set no limits at all on children and allow them total freedom of expression. Thus misguided, some parents found themselves guardians of virtually uncontrollable children—children who were actually quite unhappy because no limits whatsoever had been defined for them.

Clearly, neither extreme—neither the philosophy of regular beatings nor the notion of limitless freedom—will produce a contented, happy, self-disciplined child. Many of us who were brought up in fairly rigid households as well as those of us who were ourselves raised during the permissive era of a decade ago now feel confused about just how strict or liberal we should be. Brought up to believe, in many cases, that corporal punishment was the most efficient and sensible way to discipline a child, yet having heard through the media and from friends that there might be other, better, ways of rearing our children, we often feel at sea, trying one method this week, attempting another style of discipline the next. Even our questions reflect this basic confusion. This woman, for example, uses the words *punishment, spanking* and *discipline* interchangeably in the same paragraph:

> I just don't know what kind of discipline will work best with my four-year-old. When it comes time to punish him, his father thinks we should spank him, because that's the way he was raised. But I feel we should send my son to his room, or some other kind of punishment. I know you don't believe in spanking, but I'm confused about what other kinds of punishments work.

Although punishment and discipline are related, they are not the same. Before good discipline can take place in the home, it is important to tease out the differences between these two concepts.

To understand what is meant by discipline, I like to look at the Latin root of the word: *discipulus,* or disciple. That word best expresses the ideal relationship of child to parent. A parent acts as teacher and model, helping his child to develop self-control, character, orderly conduct, a sense of values, good judgment, empathy for human beings and other creatures and, most important, self-discipline. These are a parent's long-term goals, and it is important to bear them in mind continuously throughout the different stages of a child's development. By focusing on the long-term goals, parents will then have a philosophy on which to base their day-to-day discipline decisions. This philosophy will also help parents be consistent in dealing with their children.

Every day, however, parents are confronted with dozens of short-term goals. And it is these short-term goals that often get us into trouble when we discipline our children. Ideally, short-term goals should eventually lead to our long-term goals, such as getting a child to make a sound judgment about how much TV to watch on a given day, or getting the child to want to finish his homework assignment because he understands that it is in his best interests to do so. But all too often, our short-term goals sound like this: "Get dressed now or you're going to get it. You have to be at school and I have to be at work in ten minutes!" "That's enough TV. Turn it off!" "No, you can't have another cookie. Why? Because I said so."

The exigencies of everyday life often leave us frazzled, frustrated and quick to snap out the easiest and fastest response to a child's behavior. Frequently we want compliance and obedience, and we want it right now—but in gaining these immediate results, we may be working against our long-term goals. We may manage to stop disagreeable behavior in the here-and-now, but in so doing, we may hinder the child's attempts to learn self-discipline over the long haul. Ideally, short-term goals and long-term goals should work in tandem.

Discipline isn't just punishing, forcing compliance or stamping out bad behavior. Rather, discipline has to do with teaching proper deportment, caring about others, controlling oneself and putting someone else's wishes before one's own when the occasion calls for it. These concepts are best learned by establishing an atmosphere of *mutuality* in the family.

As a parent, you should ask yourself from time to time, "What kind of a relationship do I want with my child?" Do you want a master-and-slave relationship, or do you want a relationship built on mutual respect and love? Punishment without proper discipline will lead to the master-and-slave relationship. Discipline, as I have described it and will elaborate upon in this book, will lead to mutuality. The master-and-slave relationship may be easier in the short term. After all, if you bark an order, the child, out of fear of reprisal, is likely to obey you, making your job seem simple. But achieving this short-term goal by threats or punishment may make your more important long-term goals virtually impossible to reach.

Mutual respect doesn't mean that all members of the family are equal, however. They are not. Small children are small children, and adults are adults. Young children usually don't have the good judgment to make sound decisions. Nor does mutual respect mean that you won't have to lay down the law when compliance is vital—either for the child's safety or to help him move forward in life—or that you are absolved from setting clear and appropriate limits. What it *does* mean is that discipline will take place in a context of empathy, love, protection and guidance, and will provide the foundation on which the child can then build toward his most important long-term goal: self-discipline. For what is the value of discipline if the end result is not self-discipline?

As a parent, you will also want to instill in your child self-confidence, self-control and self-esteem. Integral parts of the discipline process, these valued attributes can be damaged or lost altogether if your child is made to feel, through excessively harsh punishments, that he or she is a bad person. A child who feels miserable or, worse, thinks he ought to be miserable because of the way he has been treated, may begin to believe that he has no right to self-esteem or self-confidence. In addition, because he may never have been encouraged to develop self-discipline, he may grow into an adult who has little or no control over his actions.

It is my contention that discipline takes place in a positive context, and punishment in a more negative one. Sometimes mild punishments are necessary in the overall scheme of disciplining your child in order to show him that certain actions may bring unpleasant consequences. But unless these punishments take place within the larger, more positive context of discipline, they will not be effective and may, indeed, be harmful to the child.

Of course, no family lives in isolation. Whenever we talk about discipline, we have to consider the values of the culture that surrounds us. If the culture values independent and self-reliant adults, then one goal for parents will be to help their children achieve these attributes. If the culture values respect for elders above all else, discipline in the home will probably reflect this value. Because of the heterogeneous and multi-class nature of our society, many different sets of cultural values exist even within one small area. The values of your class, ethnic group, family and even geographical location (urban versus rural, for instance) may affect the lessons that you teach your children and the manner in which you choose to discipline them.

CRITICAL MOMENTS

Discipline takes place continuously, during a series of critical moments when the needs and desires of your child come into conflict with either your short-term or long-term goals. To best understand these critical moments and to be better able to handle them, it is first necessary to know what governs your child during a given stage of his development so that you can put your expectations in line with his capabilities.

In this book, I will be talking about five stages of development: infancy, toddlerhood, preschool age, school age and the preteen years. As I examine these different stages, I will discuss what the child is capable of morally, emotionally, socially and cognitively at each level of development, and will suggest what disciplinary goals might be appropriate for each particular age. Often a parent's confusion about discipline stems from a lack of understanding about what the child is capable of doing. To punish a three-year-old for telling a lie, for example, would be counterproductive, since at preschool age he is just learning to distinguish right from wrong. To reprimand a toddler for not sitting still in a restaurant would be futile, since a toddler hasn't reached a stage of development that allows him to sit still for any length of time. Of course, not all children are the same in any given stage of development. Some are docile and obedient by nature; others seem especially willful and resistant. But the better you understand what your child can do at a particular age and attune your expectations to his development, the easier it will be to discipline him.

For the most part, young children up to the age of eighteen months are innocent of willful acts of disobedience and defiance. Any punishment at this age would be inappropriate. A thirteen-month-old finds an electric socket fascinating. You shake your head *no*. The child looks at you, shakes her head *no*, and continues to play with the socket. Your first thought might be that the child is defying you. But she isn't. She simply doesn't know the rules of the game yet. The healthy child is a curious child, an experimenting child. If exploration takes her into areas you deem dangerous or off-limits, then you have to convey this to her in a fashion that won't impede her further development or squash her curiosity. The job of a parent is to aid the child in developing an accurate perception of reality, but this must be done without threatening the child's self-esteem.

A toddler is, by definition, negative. She turns your world topsy-turvy. No matter what you want a toddler to do, she wants to do the opposite. She's actually looking to pick a fight. In the section on toddlers, I will explain the reasons for this maddening behavior and will try to help you set up two major goals during this stage. The first is simply figuring out how to survive this trying period. The second and, of course, more important, is helping the toddler learn how to negotiate her environment. A toddler needs to learn how to break loose from you and yet still feel secure in your presence. Once you can live with this concept, much of the toddler's seemingly inexplicable behavior will appear to be more logical.

Preschool children are more sophisticated than toddlers. They want to be like you and try out many of the prerogatives of adults, often leading to bouts of competition as to who is boss. Your goal as a parent is to nurture the child's desire to be a self-starter and help him begin to adopt some of your attitudes and values, but without humiliating the child or suppressing his newfound assertiveness. During this period, the child is acquiring skills that he will need in order to be an adult one day. He is developing the beginnings of a value system and moral judgment. Your goal is to turn your child into a sidekick, to help him and teach him along the way, rather than to be overly punitive and risk becoming enemies because you're always in conflict.

The parent of a school-age child has other worries. Peer and teacher influences have a strong impact on the child, who must also grapple with schoolwork as well as social pressures to belong to a group. Your goal during this age is to help the child become more independent and practice exercising good judgment, to help her develop a firm sense of self so that she will not be persuaded by others to get into trouble, and to help her learn to conform socially when it is desirable.

One of the central issues for preteens—eleven- and twelve-year-olds —is preparation for sexual maturity and the responsibility that goes with it. That's where the parent comes in—as a guide and as a teacher during this important time. For a child, the preteen years also represent something of a paradox: At the same time that he is demonstrating greater involvement with friends and developing social interests outside the home, he also has a very strong sense of belonging to the family. At the very moment the child begins to break away from the family, his need for the security it offers becomes especially strong. But his relationship to the family should include responsibility to the family unit. For a preteen this ought to translate into chores, integrating his needs into the family's needs and learning to be a responsible consumer.

Once you, as a parent, understand your child's various levels of development, the next step is to have at your disposal a number of age-appropriate techniques that will help the disciplining process. The form of discipline I prefer, and will stress in subsequent chapters, is anticipation and preparedness on the part of the parent, rather than punishment of the child after an infraction. Perhaps the motto ought to be: Prevention rather than punishment. You can avoid a number of problems if you learn to anticipate a child's undesirable behavior and give some forethought as to how you will deal with the situation.

Cutting the child off at the pass won't always be possible, but there are many other discipline strategies. Techniques that I will elaborate upon throughout the book include telling the child the consequences of his behavior ahead of time, reasoning with him, teaching him how to negotiate, distracting him from undesirable behavior, cajoling, compromising, providing alternatives, picking your battles, instituting democratic procedures and using humor and the cold shoulder.

I will also discuss how to make the discipline suitable to the occasion. For example, sending a child to his room because he forgot to bring his bicycle in from the rain after he was repeatedly asked to do so might not make much sense. Telling the child, however, that he will not be permitted to ride the bicycle for a certain period of time does make sense. In this way, the parent is teaching the child a real-life lesson in preparation for adulthood: If we do not care for our belongings, we may find that we can no longer use them. In other words, punishment should relate logically to the situation. Some further examples include telling a child she can't have a snack after dinner because she ate one when she wasn't supposed to, teaching a young child the consequences of breaking his crayons by not replacing them immediately, and not allowing an older child to attend an evening recreational event because he did not honor a mutually agreed upon curfew the night before.

CORPORAL PUNISHMENT

One discipline technique that I do not approve of, as I am sure will already be apparent, is corporal punishment. Shaming, humiliating and beating a child are, at the very least, counterproductive. Corporal punishment is an abuse of power. It suggests that might makes right and actually encourages a child to do the same.

One of my earliest memories is of an afternoon when I was staying with my grandmother. Often when I visited her, she would put a cushion on the windowsill, where we would sit together and look out at all the activity on the street. It was a very peaceful time for me, being with her and watching the world go by. One afternoon, however, the girl from across the street, whom I had seen playing out front, must have done something she shouldn't have, because her mother appeared at the front steps of their apartment building and began screaming at her. The girl was only five or six years old, and I have no idea what it was she had done, but I remember that the mother's appearance took me by surprise. Then to my horror, the mother ran out to where the little girl was playing and began dragging her by the hair right down the middle of the street—not even on the sidewalk. The girl was shrieking at the top of her lungs; the mother was screaming and yelling and hitting the child with her free hand. The scene was so terrifying to me at the time that I remember it made me sick to my stomach. It was my first encounter with violent punishment.

Over the years I have had occasion to witness other instances of what I feel were inappropriate and excessive uses of physical punishment. Once while waiting for someone on a corner near where I now live and watching for him down the street, I saw a mother and her five-year-old son walking toward me. The mother was pushing a stroller with a baby in it. When they reached the middle of the block, the little boy, who had been walking dutifully beside his mother, suddenly had an attack of high spirits and began skipping rather than walking. To my astonishment, the mother swung her hand in a forceful motion, smacked the child right across the mouth and barked at him, "Walk straight!" The child didn't cry. He must have been used to being smacked in that way. But the most bitter, angry and murderous expression came over his face. Then he quickly grimaced at his mother when he knew she wasn't looking, and they continued on their way.

Another time, while shopping in a supermarket, I noticed a child who was pretending to skate down the aisle between the groceries. He was having a fine time and was, I observed, managing to thread his way deftly among the shoppers. His mother was standing in the aisle with a full cart of groceries and chatting with another woman. As the boy glided past her, she reached out and hit him against his bare thighs. I didn't hear what she said, but I guessed that she told him she didn't want him to do that anymore. The boy looked up and noticed that I was watching. The expression on his face was a mixture of bravery—he was trying to hold back the tears—and rebelliousness. He had been humiliated, but with that one look seemed to be saying, "She can't make me cry."

As a psychologist in private practice, I've had similar stories recounted to me by patients. One man told me that when he was a child his mother would chase after him with a big wooden ladle, and that he would actually have to run out of the house and into the yard to get away from her. He remembers his mother as someone who terrorized him. Another man told how his aunt, who baby-sat for him when he was a youngster, would methodically line up all the children in the bathroom at the end of the day for punishment. She would sit on the toilet-seat cover as if it were a throne and mete out this "justice" by making them take their pants down, putting them across her knee and smacking them on their buttocks with a hairbrush.

As a child-care specialist on call-in radio programs in the New York City area and nationwide, I have also heard countless stories of corporal punishment from confused and distraught parents who are troubled by their own methods of discipline, mostly because they don't seem to work very well. Among the scores of such phone calls, one in particular stands out in my mind. The mother of a five-year-old boy called to say that she was embroiled in a very difficult situation. Her son, according to her description, had a very bad temper. To control it, she and her husband had tried everything: They had hit the boy, yelled at him, locked him in his room and then locked him out of the house. This last move seemed to be the proverbial straw that broke the camel's back. The little boy, by now very reactive, was breaking windows and the glass on the front door with his bare hands. That image was a sad and horrifying one. Discipline in that particular family had simply gotten out of hand and had escalated to a point where it was going to require a tremendous amount of patience, skill and love to get it back under control.

In principle, I am against all the forms of punishment this mother used to try to control her son: hitting, yelling and locking the child in his room and then out of the house. I have even heard of parents locking children in closets as a form of punishment. At times, a parent might choose to isolate a child for some misbehavior. But if you are going to banish your child to his room, it should be for a short time only. A responsible parent will monitor the child's behavior rather than rely on the jail-cell approach.

Excessive yelling will prove inhumane and ineffective in the long run, too. By and large, a conversational tone keeps everybody calm. Once in a while, however, when a major disagreement erupts, raised voices are certainly understandable. Screaming is a natural reaction, even though a deep firm tone is likely to be more influential. A constant diet of yelling can cause children to become anxious, to disregard verbal commands and to stop listening, and can even provoke some children to proceed further with bad behavior.

Sarcasm is also ineffectual—and may be destructive as well. Sarcasm is a form of hostility expressed as a biting comment, just as a child sometimes bites another child or an adult out of anger. Sarcasm can be particularly damaging for young children because it's so confusing. If you say to a child, "Well, that was really nice!" when you actually mean, "That was horrid," he is confronted with an inconsistency between your words and your meaning. This kind of ambiguous message can be very perplexing to a child who has not yet developed sophisticated thought processes. Young children are incapable of understanding irony, figures of speech and metaphors.

Spanking, constant yelling and screaming, and hostile sarcasm are all examples of poor discipline. At its worst, poor discipline leads to violence, which, in turn, leads to child abuse. From 1976 to 1984, reports of child abuse in this country increased by 156 percent, in most instances stemming from parents taking out their anger on their children. Experts tell us that child abuse is rising by 9 percent a year and that two million cases of bruises, broken bones and burns are reported to the authorities annually (many other cases go unreported). On the rise, too, is the number of child-abuse centers where parents can go for help. There, the major message social workers and psychologists try to teach parents is that there *is* a way to discipline a child without hitting him.

Many parents resort to spanking, humiliation and threats to get their children to behave, either because they are ignorant of the various ways to impose sensible, humane and reasonable discipline, or because they are unable to get their own reactions under control.

With the breakdown of the extended family and the subsequent scarcity of family members from whom to seek advice, many new parents feel alone and somewhat lost. They are confused about the right thing to do, baffled by the often relentless demands of their infants and occasionally even enraged by their children's behavior. Consequently, this rage sometimes comes to the fore and causes them to resort to the quickest method of discipline that springs to mind: the punishing slap or the threat of one.

Even parents who have access to the advice of other family members and are mindful of other, more effective and more humane ways of disciplining children still find that they can't get rid of the legacy of corporal punishment with which they themselves were raised. Here are the comments of one woman I spoke to:

> It has been a real reach for me to be a different kind of parent than my own parents were. I have very vivid memories of being terrorized by the fear of being spanked by my father. I remember fooling around with my brothers in the bedroom early in the morning, and seeing my father, furious at us for making so much noise, come barreling through the door, smacking everything in his way. I have awful memories of being in the backseat of the car, and his hand swinging around at us as we were playing. I remember that it was a rule in my house that I had to be in the door by five o'clock, or else I didn't get any dinner. If I got in five minutes late, that was just too bad. I went to bed hungry.
>
> Now I have my own little boy, and when he does something that infuriates me, I feel this tremendous urge to spank him and be done with it. I know in my head that it's not the right thing to do, but in my gut, I want to hit him.
>
> I remember that I had this same feeling as a high school teacher when I was just starting out. I was twenty-one and had no experience disciplining anybody, but there I was up in front of thirty students. And to my surprise, I became a drill sergeant. I heard my father's voice coming out of me, and it was like *The Three Faces of Eve*. When this voice comes out of you, you don't know where it's coming from, and it's tough, terrifically tough.
>
> For me it's been hard to be an intelligent parent, an intelligent disciplinarian, because I feel as if I'm straining against the grain of my natural instincts when I try to stay calm, to find ways to distract my son, not just to yell or hit or demand blind obedience. It's had to be the triumph of my brain over my emotions.
>
> I feel this legacy so strongly. It was especially apparent to me when I would go to visit my parents and I would be more punitive

toward my son than I was at home, because I felt that I had to show
them that I was a good parent according to their rules, and that I
wasn't letting him "get away with anything." And I would feel sick
about it, and guilty and sad for him, because for him, it was coming
out of nowhere.

The conscious or unconscious legacy of corporal punishment, the
dearth of wise elders to go to for good advice and the lack of parental
education about discipline have all contributed to an atmosphere of
confusion and distress for many parents faced with the desire to do the
right thing for their children and to help them grow into happy, healthy
and responsible adults.

THE EFFECTS OF CORPORAL PUNISHMENT

Children who are regularly treated with excessive punitiveness learn to
become immune to pain. You often hear them say so as they grow older:
"Okay, hit me. I won't cry." This is not a desirable consequence, because in the process of learning to steel themselves against pain, they
become a little less human. They learn to shut off their emotions and
become more mechanical beings.

Such treatment also has the undesirable effect of hindering a child's
ability to develop an inner sense of morality. If a child can learn to
cope with the external punishment that's coming—if there is always a
"policeman" ready to punish him for doing something wrong—how
can he develop an internal sense of judgment or morality? In such a
system, morality becomes something that is outside the child and is
imposed upon him, not something that develops from within. If he gets
caught, he gets punished. If he doesn't get caught, what's the problem?

A child who has been abused may also become callous. As he becomes immune to the abuse, he may learn to become immune to the
pain of other individuals as well, losing his capacity for sensitivity and
empathy.

Humiliation can have disastrous consequences for some children as
they grow into adults and try to form relationships. If a child gets accustomed to a loved one smacking him around or humiliating him, he may
as an adult choose relationships in which he will continue to be abused
and humiliated. The abuse this child is used to receiving from the person who loves him and on whom he depends becomes his given, setting

up a pattern that will be difficult to break, just as the legacy of corporal punishment made it hard for the woman who inherited it to be an intelligent disciplinarian.

It is obvious that child abuse has many terrible side effects and horrendous lasting consequences. By now it is fairly well documented that children who are physically abused by their parents will probably grow into abusive parents themselves. There are also more subtle but profound consequences, however. In my clinical experience, two trends have emerged that are not often cited.

One is that the abused child believes he actually deserves the beatings and humiliation, a distortion born of immaturity and dependency. The child whose integrity is violated in this way tends to engage in self-punitive actions and thoughts. These can take many forms: provocative behavior that elicits punishment, self-mutilation, thoughts of suicide and suicide attempts, to mention just a few. Although I do not have scientific evidence to support a general theory, I have come to believe that many adolescent suicides are the consequence of childhood physical and/or mental abuse. The hopelessness and low self-esteem that can result from such treatment, coupled with an overwhelming sense of guilt, can easily lead a vulnerable teenager to the terrible decision to put a permanent end to the emotional anguish.

The other derailment I have noticed occurs in the realm of sexual development. Simply put, physical beatings can become linked with sexual arousal, even in small children. This, of course, has many unfortunate consequences. For some, it may mean that being touched cannot be experienced as affection. It is almost impossible for such children to give or receive physical demonstrations of affection. For others, sadism and masochism may become the prevailing themes in their adult interpersonal relationships. They feel alive or aroused only if there is an element of hostility or actual pain. Although I have limited clinical experience with adults who are child sexual offenders, I am inclined to think that, for many, the compulsion is due to the emotional trauma caused by physical beatings in their own early childhood. Childhood abuse may be the unrecognized source of many other adult personality problems.

We must be mindful that along with consistent corporal punishment goes an immeasurable amount of emotional battering. That which masquerades as a means to instill respect for authority may be nothing more than a cruel self-serving deception that hides a sadistic motivation.

Of course, not every parent who occasionally spanks a child is abusive. In fact, my guess is that it would be pretty rare to find a parent who had never once given a child even a little slap. As in all behavior, there are gradations, and the gradations matter. Let me explain.

Let's say you have tried just about everything you can think of and still can't get your child to cooperate with you. Your child is miserable and cranky and very resistant, so you decide to put him down in his room for a minute. As you carry him, he pulls your hair or scratches or pinches you. Tired, angry and frustrated, your final response is to say, "Just sit there and keep quiet," and spank the child on the bottom. Although I think it would be better to omit the hitting, in this context I don't consider such a reaction abusive treatment. After a while, you might say calmly to the child, "I don't want you to hit me and I don't want to hit you, so let's just stop the hitting. That's not the answer."

That situation is quite different from the one described by a parent I spoke with recently, who said she had to threaten her girls with a stick to get them to do anything. Before even trying other options, she resorted immediately to threatening and hitting. If alternatives are absent in a relationship, the relationship becomes adversarial. If threats and hits and screams are the only means of discipline, the relationship becomes abusive.

SETTING LIMITS

Disciplining your children must include setting appropriate limits for them. Without limits a child may suffer serious consequences. For example, a child who gets away with too much may feel as if he doesn't deserve his good fortune, and as a result may be plagued by feelings of guilt. The absence of limits can also produce terrible feelings of anxiety in some children, because they fear they will spiral out of control. Insatiable greed is another possible result. A child whose parents don't set limits for him will never learn to do so for himself, and will never feel as if he's had enough of anything. If there is never a limit, then there can never be a sense of satisfaction at having reached it. Another child may grow up believing that he is a fraud. Because he constantly gets away with undesirable behavior, he never feels he's earned the good things that have come his way and may develop a sense of being inauthentic or fake—of having an identity that doesn't feel quite real.

A child who worries too much about spiraling out of control may become precociously self-reliant, unconsciously setting limits for himself that are too harsh and repressive. Such inhibition may prevent him from exploring his creativity and may stunt his emotional growth. Finally, a lack of limits also makes it nearly impossible for a child to learn to follow directions comfortably, which can have very profound consequences during the school years and, indeed, for all of his life. Uncontrolled, a child's impulses become unruly and don't allow him to conform or pay attention to another's words. The inability to listen to instructions makes learning difficult.

REPAIRING THE RELATIONSHIP

An adversarial relationship prevents a child and his parent from spending calm, peaceful time together. In a master-and-slave relationship, time spent together will lack richness and dimension. Tension and the fear of becoming embroiled in a contest makes just taking a stroll together and examining a caterpillar on a branch, for example, nearly impossible. As a parent, you want to be able to say to your child, "Let's look at that caterpillar. Do you want to pick it up? You have to be very gentle and not hurt it . . ." and so on, not, "Don't touch that caterpillar!"

A parent who has already created an adversarial relationship with his child and wants to break the cycle of hitting and threatening will have to be very courageous. It requires you to recognize that violent reaction is not desirable, and that something has to be changed. It requires you to examine at the end of the day everything that took place between you and your child and to look at whatever may have triggered the desire to hit or yell. Once those triggers are identified, you can then ask yourself how you might have acted sooner to prevent the tension from reaching the level that made you lash out.

Should something trigger rage in you, take a second to say to yourself, "I have to stop right now. It doesn't matter what my child is doing; I don't want to smack him as I have done countless times in the past." Drop your voice dramatically and say to the child, "I don't want to get into this with you again," then turn around and leave the room. As you are leaving, talk to yourself: "We nearly got to the point of no return. He triggered off a reaction in me. I feel like spanking him because he won't listen to me. There has got to be another way." Meanwhile, you have killed a minute or two and given your anger a chance to cool off.

Some people use other methods: turning on the radio, getting a drink of water. If these don't work, get on the phone and call a friend. Say, "I've run out of options, and I feel like smacking my kid." But however you do it, your goal is to exercise self-control. In many ways, ridding yourself of the impulse to spank is like ridding yourself of any other undesirable habit—smoking, overeating, drinking.

Discipline doesn't exist in a vacuum. If your life is fraught with tensions caused by health or financial problems or marital stress, your ability to guide and protect your child effectively as a parent will be limited. Not only will these other issues distract you from dealing with your child, but also, stress makes it very easy to take out your frustrations on him. Again, self-control is the issue.

WHEN PARENTS DISAGREE

Parental disagreement about how to handle a child in a specific situation directly impinges on discipline. Each parent can have an individual style of interacting with a child—for example, one parent may be more physical with the child than the other, horsing around and playing active games. Research indicates that fathers treat their children in somewhat different physical and social ways than mothers do, and a child will intuit these subtle differences. But in broader respects, parents should present a united front. Sharing a philosophy of and the responsibility for child rearing will make life a lot easier for the child.

An occasional disagreement is not the end of the world. The question is, how do you deal with it? How is it going to be expressed? How is it going to be resolved?

It's best to keep the disagreement private and out of the child's earshot. Parents should work out matters of discipline between themselves and try to reach some mutual solution without dragging the child into it. Unfortunately, in the heat of an argument you are probably not going to be that tactful or think about the child's interests, and you may find yourself yelling and screaming at each other in front of him. This is bad for several reasons. One, the child will be torn apart immediately by feelings of divided loyalty. Two, it scares the life out of a child to see his parents angry with each other, because he doesn't know what is going to happen to him. Three, it frightens him to wonder what is going to happen if his parents lose control. Are they going to explode or disappear from the face of the earth?

If you find yourself in disagreement in front of a young child, I would suggest letting one parent handle it on the spot. Later on, after the child has gone to bed, discuss the matter. You might say to your spouse, "Hey, this afternoon, you handled the situation in a way I don't think was absolutely fair," or "I think you should have been stronger about it," or "You let him get away with something he shouldn't have." Work out between yourselves how to handle it the next time, because, almost certainly, there will be a next time.

When the child gets older (into the school-age and preteen years), you can invite him to join you in a discussion of certain discipline situations. You might say to the child, "Hey, yesterday I lost my temper and punished you. I grounded you for a week. All right, that happened. Now let's sit down together, you and Dad and I, and figure out what to do if this comes up again so that we don't just automatically fly off the handle and ground you again." Or you might say, if you and your spouse disagree on how to handle a situation, "Mom has one idea and Dad has another, and we are both trying to figure out a really good way to deal with you on this." That way, you won't let the child divide you, and the child won't have to worry that you are being divided.

Many parents make the mistake of leaving the discipline to the absent parent. "Wait until Daddy gets home!" has become a cliché. But as one distraught father said to me recently, "When do I ever get to love my kids? When do I ever get to hug my kids if I have to discipline them the moment I walk in the door?"

My answer is that the parent in charge is the disciplinarian. If that person is the mother most of the day, then it should be her responsibility to discipline the child on the spot. I do not believe in letting discipline wait for another parent to handle it, nor do I think the father or mother should be allowed to become a shadowy figure who walks in the door and has to play the bad guy in the house. Whoever is there is in charge. If the child is in your care and you feed him and bathe him, you are also in charge of whatever discipline is necessary. (The American family is changing, however. Today, dual-career, dual-income families represent the majority, and it's no longer just Dad who walks through the door at the end of a long day. A discussion of how to talk to a surrogate caregiver about discipline appears in the chapter Special Considerations.)

THE BASIC TENETS OF GOOD DISCIPLINE

Throughout this book I provide examples of common discipline problems that parents must deal with daily. I hope most of the situations will relate to ones you are experiencing, and that you will find my answers helpful. While the examples are fairly specific, you should be able to generalize from my illustrations and apply the solutions I suggest to your own discipline problems. I believe that the particular ideas that have helped shape my own thinking will help you guide and assist your child toward greater autonomy and self-discipline.

An Opportunity to Practice

Have you taken a course since you became a parent? Perhaps a workshop on computers or a series of driving lessons? Weren't you glad you practiced and made your mistakes on someone else's equipment? Well, children don't have the luxury of that special kind of setting in which to practice the new skills they are learning every day. Where are they to learn from their mistakes, as the saying goes, if they don't have the opportunity to do so at home?

You will find that you'll need to build into your life-style and budget something known in inventory lingo as "breakage." Wanton destruction is not acceptable, but prudent measures of freedom are absolutely necessary. For example, when a child is learning how to pour, parents must not only provide appropriate vessels and adequate instructions, but also must understand that spillage is unavoidable. On these terms a home can be a wonderfully supportive and encouraging training ground.

Try not to be too restrictive or inhibiting. At times breakage is its own punishment. Occasionally a child will accidentally damage a toy or a game or a special article of clothing. Not having the item is the logical result and may be enough of a lesson. You needn't add to her dismay by accusing her of wrongdoing. A mild statement should suffice, along with some suggestions about how to repair the item, if possible.

Serving as an Example

As a parent, you will often serve as an inadvertent example to your child. A child will model himself after you in many areas: how you deal with frustration, settle disagreements and cope with not being able to have the things that you want, to name just three.

Do you ever swear when you are angry? Well, then, when you hear your children swearing, don't be surprised. Sometimes they pick up the words from playmates, but they can also get the habit from you.

Naturally, when you are in your own home environment, you can't put on an act. But I do think you have to try your best to control yourself properly. Keep in mind that the way you respond to situations is viewed by somebody else, and that little somebody else is going to imitate you. A child learns to exercise self-control not just because you tell him to, but because he witnesses how other people around him handle frustration. If you bicker constantly with your spouse about who is going to do this and who is going to do that, you can't expect your child to rise, statesmanlike, above it all. Instead, he is very likely to emulate your conduct.

Sometimes you may purposely strive to be a model for your child. For example, perhaps you see an item in a store but realize that you can't afford it now, so you forgo it. This is an excellent opportunity to teach restraint. You might say to yourself, "Hey, you know, I really wish I could get that. But it's a little too expensive. I will either wait until it goes on sale or until I have saved up enough money." In this way you show your child that you impose limits on yourself. If you can live with them, your child may find it somewhat easier to live with his own.

Pick Your Battles

Every day, there will be instances when you and your child have a difference of opinion. Interestingly, while you might be tolerant of such conflicts with a spouse, a friend or an employer, you may find that you quickly grow impatient with your child, perhaps because you feel that your power is threatened in some way.

To make life more bearable and pleasant for everybody, choose the issues that are significant enough to fight over, and ignore or use distraction for those you can let slide that day. Picking your battles will eliminate a number of conflicts, and yet will still leave you feeling in control. You will have been the one to decide which confrontations were important. You won't feel that your child is taking advantage of you or has manipulated you.

I recommend that at the end of the day you find some time to be alone to review the day's events. Jot down the battles you had with your child. After you've compiled a list, review it to see if some were avoidable and determine which were really worth the fight. This will be good preparation for the next day, when, in all likelihood, the same conflicts will emerge. Then, however, you'll be ready with a strategy and can be selective about your skirmishes.

Parental Expectations and Children's Capabilities

Very often in a discipline situation we are tempted to punish our children because they are not going along with something we want. But occasionally our expectations are out of line with what the child is capable of doing. For example, if you expect your eight-month-old son to entertain himself in a playpen, you'll probably both end up feeling frustrated, since most children that age can't play by themselves for any length of time. You may be tempted to punish him for not doing so. The same holds true when you expect a toddler to sit still in a restaurant or an infant to resist putting things in his mouth, or when you expect a preschooler to be neat or polite to relatives. Demanding the impossible is destined to lead to frustration. Rather, I would like you to ask yourself as you manage these daily issues: "Am I asking something of my child that he can do?"

Labeling

How many adults have you seen shame and humiliate a child by calling him a name in order to enforce discipline? Parents sometimes say to a child, "That's the dumbest thing I ever heard," or "Boy, you are really a klutz," or "a jerk," or "crazy" or "a monster."

To label a child is to do him a terrible disservice. If you call a child a name enough times, it may become a self-fulfilling prophecy. He may begin to think he really is a monster, and therefore he will behave like one. Such labeling can damage a child's self-image.

If you must label a child, I would prefer that you err on the positive side. Do avoid generalities, however. For example, try not to call a child "a good little girl." The term is not specific enough. Is she a good little girl because she obeyed her mother? Or because she spoke up against some injustice? Rather, be as descriptive and precise as possible: "You are very good at puzzles" or "you have chosen a nice outfit to wear today."

Be prudent about giving a child credit for something she has no control over. Saying something as broad as "You're very pretty" to a little girl addresses only her innate looks. I would rather you say something more concrete, such as "I like the way you did your hair today," which compliments a choice she made about her appearance. Please don't get me wrong. A compliment such as "You look beautiful" is wonderful to give and to receive. Just be mindful that there must be a balance and that the accent should be on other, self-determined attributes.

Empty Promises and Outrageous Threats

Parents may sometimes be tempted to offer children treats that they have no intention of ever giving them. This is a very poor child-rearing practice, because if you don't follow through, the child will become crushed and disappointed. Children count on promises even if you make them quite casually and don't really mean what you say. Such disappointments damage a child's ability to trust you.

Outrageous threats also damage trust and credibility. I've heard parents say to children, "I'll leave you here if you don't stop that." Now, the parent knows he really wouldn't ever leave the child. And if the parent says it often enough, the child is soon going to figure that out. More amusing is the parent who threatens, "If you don't put your shoes on, I'm going to kindergarten without you!" One parent even threatened to dismantle her child's bed and give it away to a neighbor's son. Others threaten to give away the uncooperative child. I've heard much worse, of course, and strongly urge that you resist using scare tactics as a means of control.

Bribery versus Rewards

Responsible promises can be inducements for cooperation, but trying to decide whether they are rewards or bribes can be difficult. It is a matter of interpretation as well as a matter of intent. The word *bribe* has a negative connotation and is usually associated with getting someone to do something corrupt, while the word *reward* refers to meritorious behavior. If you remember that distinction, you won't be ambivalent about offering a prize for desirable behavior.

Although rewards have their place, deciding what to offer, when, how much and how often is a complicated matter. Heavy reliance on their use can convey to a child the message that one conforms to another's wishes in order to acquire something. Moderately administered, however, rewards can motivate a child to attempt an activity or behavior she might not otherwise try. Eventually the accomplishment can be its own reward.

Heavy-handed Punishments

Although I will often urge you to think about protection and guidance rather than punishment, there are times when it may be necessary to teach your child that some actions have negative consequences. Be wary, however, of heavy-handed punishments—punishments that are mentally or physically excessive and may be oppressive to the child.

If possible, advise your child of the possible consequences of his actions before the infraction ever takes place. For example, if your child asks to ride his bike, tell him he may do so, but that if he doesn't put the bicycle away after he has ridden it, he won't be able to take it out again tomorrow.

Naturally, there will be times when no advance warning is possible because neither of you anticipated any misbehavior. In general (with the possible exception of very serious misbehavior such as vandalism), when it happens the first time, talk to the child about the action and tell him what the consequences will be if he does it again. Let's say the child took something out of your pocketbook without your permission. Say to him, "When you took that wallet out of my pocketbook without asking my permission, maybe you didn't realize it, but that belongs to me. You shouldn't take things that are my property. I'll have to ask you not to do that anymore. If it should happen again, I'm afraid I will have to take away your privilege of going to the store to buy snacks for a couple of days."

Punishments should be humane and should not involve shame or humiliation. And don't, in your frustration or anger, mete out a punishment that is not only too harsh, but is also too difficult to carry out. Grounding a child for a month is a perfect example. A month is a long time in the life of a child—or a family, for that matter. Two weeks later, the punishment may seem silly and, worse, too difficult to enforce. Doling out a punishment that you cannot enforce will make your discipline task that much harder.

Erratic and Inconsistent Handling

Erratic and inconsistent handling differs from arbitrary and inflexible handling. An inflexible parent who is unwilling to change with a child's developmental needs, to bend when necessary, or who insists on honoring the status quo regardless of the circumstances, will hurt both himself and his child, and will find that his discipline lacks a warm, humane touch. Inconsistency, however, can be just as damaging.

Let's say you have told your preschooler that she can watch one half hour of television before supper. After the half hour, she whines and cries. Yesterday, because you had your wits about you, you were able to deal with the whining and crying in a matter-of-fact manner. You simply turned off the television and invited her to join you in another activity. But today, because the phone has just rung and something is burning on the stove and the delivery man has just arrived with the new chair, you can't cope with her, and therefore you give in and tell her she can watch TV beyond the half-hour limit. This is an example of inconsistent handling. What lesson is she to learn from this? That if she can get you really frazzled, you'll give in to her?

Being flexible, however, is another matter. Let's say you have a nine-year-old son, and you have made a rule in your house that he can't go outside after dinner to play with his friends unless his homework is completed. But just as he's sitting down to do his homework, Mr. Smith, the father of one of his friends, calls up from next door and says he'd like to take the boys to a local baseball game. You have a rule. By rights your son should not be allowed to leave the house until his homework is done, but by then, Mr. Smith and his son would be long gone. What do you do? It seems to me that this is a case that calls for a little flexibility. Perhaps you and your son could negotiate a deal in which he agrees to set the alarm for an hour earlier in the morning so that he can do his work then. In this way, you can still be consistent with your general rule about homework, but you will have demonstrated flexibility as well.

Overzealous Surveillance

Sometimes we watch our children so carefully that we don't give them a chance to explore and grow. Parents who hover over their toddlers, admonishing them not to touch this and not to touch that, may create a great deal of tension and may inadvertently cause the very behavior they are trying to prevent.

I have seen many examples of overzealous surveillance. Recently, I witnessed this scene: A mother and her son were walking down the street, and as they did so, the little boy reached out and touched each parked car they passed. Every time he did this, the mother yanked his arm and yelled, "No, don't touch!" What is wrong, I wanted to ask her, with touching a parked car?

One of the worst instances I ever observed was in the home of a friend. During my visit, a woman and her six-year-old son arrived, and as we were greeting him, the boy inadvertently leaned against the door frame. All of a sudden his mother screeched, "I told you never to touch woodwork!" The boy shrank away with a humiliated look on his face. I tried to imagine what it would be like to live in a home where I could not even touch the walls.

Toddlers need constant surveillance, but they also need chances to explore. For example, if at Grandma's house your child discovers the clock and wants to touch it, be there right alongside him, let him look at it, let him touch it gently, and control his movements if need be. Then if an emergency should arise, you can snatch the clock away. But don't deny your child the opportunity to touch something interesting just because you assume he might damage it. If you are near at hand and alert to his movements, the chances of any damage should be minimal.

Finally, I urge you to keep in mind, as you love, rear and protect your children, three basic questions:

1. What are my long-term goals?
2. What are my short-term goals?
3. In whose interests am I making this discipline decision?

Without a doubt, there will be times when you make discipline decisions based on your own self-interest. Perhaps you need to get to work, which means the child must conform to your wishes; perhaps your patience has been stretched to the breaking point, and you simply need a bit of peace and quiet. While it is perfectly all right, from time to time, to make discipline decisions in your own interests, it is important not to confuse self-interest with the interests of the child. Of course, ideally, your interests would merge!

Helping a child wait for a bottle, persevere on a frustrating puzzle, tie shoelaces or spread jelly on a roll all involve discipline. Your self-control and your child's are inextricably linked. Through discipline, your goal is to help your youngster develop mastery, self-respect and hopefulness. Discipline does not have to be a battlefield. Rather, you should think of it as the nurturing of a loving relationship in which empathy and support are the central motifs.

INFANTS:
THE BEGINNINGS OF SELF-DISCIPLINE

Not too long ago, I was having a snack in a cafeteria in an airport and happened to look over at a family sitting near me. The mother and father had just reached their table and were opening juice containers and unwrapping sandwiches, while their son, who appeared to be about nine months old, sat in a high chair next to them. Perhaps overtired from the traveling and certainly impatient with his parents' failure to feed him fast enough, the baby began to cry in frustration. Suddenly the father, perhaps overtired and hungry himself, raised his open hand and held it menacingly in front of the baby's face. "Quiet!" he yelled at the baby. "You want another one of these?"

The scene was troubling to me for several reasons. First, I am always dismayed when I see a parent raise a hand to threaten a child, because, as I have discussed in the previous chapter, I believe that hitting a child is neither effective nor humane. And in this case, the father's phrase "another one of these" seemed to imply that the child—an infant—had been hit before, perhaps often. Also troubling, however, was the fact that the father seemed not to understand the source of the child's crying.

37

Did he really believe that the crying necessitated punitive action? Did he think his small son was capable of sitting quietly in a chair when tired, and of not uttering a peep in spite of his hunger? Did he imagine that a nine-month-old child could tolerate that degree of frustration?

Much of what contrives to create such critical moments in parenting stems from a fundamental misunderstanding as to what the child is capable of at any given age. If a parent misjudges a child's limitations as well as his or her own abilities, the potential exists for unreasonable expectations, frustration, disappointment and an unrealistic belief that what the child really needs is to be punished. This seems particularly common with infants. Let's take crying as an example.

The baby in the airport cafeteria cried because that is what nine-month-olds do when they are tired and hungry. With very rare exceptions, they are not capable of doing anything else. More to the point, from birth an infant learns that crying is a remarkably effective way of getting what he wants. When the child is hungry, he cries, and you feed him. When he is uncomfortable, you cuddle him and give him a sense of security and warmth. He cries not because he is "spoiled" or "bratty" or "bad," but because he has learned, via your responses, that he has a vital impact on his environment. Unable to speak, the baby nevertheless develops effective communication by employing the one means at his disposal.

To ignore this cry on the theory that attending to it will "spoil" the child is a little silly. Even if the baby were able to control his crying, which he isn't, what would that teach him? That he is powerless? That he has no effect on his environment? That if he is uncomfortable or hungry, he can't make his situation better? To prolong this frustration and sense of powerlessness can sometimes have unfortunate effects on a growing child. If you allow an infant to feel miserable, he may grow up with the idea that somehow he deserves to feel that way. A child needs to feel comfortable and good about himself and his environment to be able to grow up with the idea that he is a good person. If he is denied that opportunity because his mother or father believed that attending to all his needs would somehow "spoil" him, it may be difficult for him to develop adequate self-esteem and self-confidence later in life.

As the child grows older you can help him learn to tolerate his frustrations—for a few minutes at first, and then later for longer periods—as part of your long-term goal to help him acquire self-discipline. But this presupposes that you understand your child's capabilities at every stage of his development. Under the best of circumstances, the father in the airport might have been able to help his child tolerate a delay of fifteen minutes by distracting him or humoring him; a nine-month-old can cope with very small delays if they are well handled, but not if he's tired and hungry. An infant's sense of time is undeveloped. A baby doesn't know the difference between a short period and a long period. He knows only the moment. Anticipating how long a wait is going to be is impossible for a child at this age. His mind is occupied only by such thoughts as, "My stomach is empty and I'm hungry," or "I just don't feel right," or "I have a tooth popping out of my gum—how long is this going to go on?" You can't reason with an infant, and he certainly can't reason with himself. Ignoring a child's cries at that point is intolerable to him, and his lack of effect on you will probably make him very angry. Raising your hand to him—*punishing* him for communicating on the only level he can—will only increase his misery.

Children grow and develop at a faster rate during the first eighteen-month period than at any other time in their lives. A three-month-old is a vastly different creature from an eighteen-month-old. Keep in mind, too, that children are born with very different temperaments. Not all three-month-olds are alike, nor are all eighteen-month-olds. Some babies are quite passive and appear to be "better behaved" than others who are more active and demanding. Still other babies appear to have what we call "colic" and are, for the first several months at least, often cranky and resistant to our attempts to make them happy. With so many variations and changes in infancy, it is difficult to make hard and fast statements about behavior, but I can offer a few helpful basics.

Three Months

In general, I wouldn't have any expectations for a child three months old or younger. I wouldn't hope for compliance any more than I would expect the infant to be able to tolerate time delays in getting what he wants. The parent of a three-month-old can expect no cooperation from the helpless baby and must be prepared to attend to the baby's needs more or less constantly. He needs to be made comfortable—fed, burped, picked up and held—and you, as the parent, will be associated with this feeling of comfort. Forget entirely any notions of "spoiling" a baby at this age. The more you are able to look after his needs, the better off the child will be both now and later on.

Six Months

By six months of age, a baby can be expected to recognize certain people familiar to her and to anticipate becoming involved with them. She should also be distractible to some extent and able to laugh at things that amuse her. This will come more easily if the parent has taken pains to encourage the child very gradually to enjoy her environment, and insured that she has not been frustrated too often or for too long. A frustrated child is a reactive child—and it's a lot easier to get compliance from a child who isn't terribly reactive. An infant who is used to having her needs quickly attended to will be more likely, over the long haul, to respond nicely later when you have to say to her, "Do me a favor. Can you wait just a second? I'll be there in a minute." The child knows that time after time you really do come to her in a minute, and because she trusts that expectation, she is able to comply with your request.

I wouldn't, however, go so far as to expect a six-month-old to be able to control herself or to look frustration in the eye and tolerate it. The parent's duty is still to soften the baby's frustration.

Nine Months

A nine-month-old child enters a very different phase of development. On one hand, a baby between the ages of nine and twelve months may be exceptionally clingy, crying miserably at the least suggestion of independence from his mother. On the other hand, a nine-month-old is a mobile baby, able to crawl around, pick himself up and shortly, if not already, able to walk.

Let's deal with the issue of clinginess first. Many parents, misunderstanding this phase of development, think that their baby is "spoiled" because he won't let Mom out of his sight. He wants Mom, and only Mom, to hold him and carry him around so he can look out the window, and doesn't want Mom to leave the room because he worries that she might disappear. To try to control a nine-month-old's clinginess by forcing him away is a mistake, because it counteracts a normal part of the child's development. To think that the child is clinging to you because he is spoiled is nonsense. Clinginess is not a discipline issue, at least not in the sense of correcting a wrongdoing. Obviously you do need to help the child separate from you, but it must be done in a thoughtful manner, as part of the child's growth and development—not as a punishment. To resist your child in such a tender and sensitive matter could have serious long-term consequences for the child: he may lose his stable base and source of security; he may feel helpless and abandoned or left behind; and he may experience a heightened separation anxiety. Separation must be gradual.

With mobility comes the need to protect the child from hazards in the home and occasionally to guard your own and others' property from him. Many parents, however, labor under the misapprehension that an infant can be taught self-control and can resist temptation. Such expectations are unreasonable and can lead to an unnecessary series of spats. Let me give you an example.

A while ago, I saw a man on a city street with a ten-month-old boy. The child held onto his father's finger for security at the same time that he was intensely interested in exploring every little piece of the environment. In this case, the boy had spied a cigarette butt on the sidewalk and was absolutely determined to touch the fascinating object. A child this age wants to reach for things that are interesting, but unlike the parents, he has no idea that there might be something wrong with picking up a cigarette butt. The immediate temptation to touch it is far more powerful than any admonition not to. In fact, such warnings are virtually meaningless to a ten-month-old child.

Such was the case with the boy and his father. The child kept bending down to try to pick up the cigarette butt. Every time he did this, the father would yank his arm. The boy would stop for a second, then look down and reach again. Finally, the father began slapping the boy's hand. Unable to resist temptation, however, the child reached down one more time. The father slapped his hand again and the boy started to cry.

Now it seems to me that the logical solution to this problem would have been to pick up the cigarette butt and throw it away. In other words, *intervene*. Get rid of the source of temptation. Once you understand that a child this age finds everything irresistible, your own task becomes clearer. Instead of scolding the child for something he has no control over, remove the object from his view. If the child realizes that the cigarette butt has been thrown away, the parent should progress from intervention to *distraction*—drawing the child's attention away from the object of his desire and toward something he will find equally fascinating, something the parent will not find so undesirable.

Hitting a ten-month-old boy will not stop him from succumbing to temptation. Until the child acquires judgment, he is going to yield to whatever piques his interest. The parent's only recourse, then, is to intervene, to distract and, if possible, to *anticipate* such temptations and remove them from the child's vicinity. Protecting a ten-month-old child is hard work and requires a tremendous amount of patience. Understanding what he can and can't do and working within those limitations will bring greater dividends as the child matures than will simply demanding obedience and forcing a baffled baby into submission.

Twelve to Eighteen Months

An infant's first birthday is a big milestone in any family. Besides the symbolic importance of the event, this age brings with it increased mobility and an expanding interest in the world. By the time a baby is a year old he is eating with his hands, sampling new foods, using a cup more frequently and interacting with other children and animals. He is just beginning to taste the allure of freedom—and this may lead to conflicts.

If a fifteen-month-old breaks away from your grip and runs wildly up the street, wanting desperately for you to run after him and then screams with glee when you do, his behavior may seem mischievous. In essence, however, the child is exhibiting a mixture of carefree abandon coupled with the emotional need for you to scoop him up protectively in your arms. It becomes a game in which he is reassured that he cannot get away from you. He is almost compelled to act this way. It may feel like defiance to you, but the child's motive is part of an entirely different, underlying drama. A painful viselike grip or a smack is not the answer. Rather, understanding that your authority is not being challenged may help you be more tolerant. This isn't to say that you shouldn't be protective. I have known some parents to say, "Let him go. If he falls down the steps he'll learn his lesson." This mean-spirited attitude grows out of frustration and is, in a sense, neglect, if not outright abuse, by omission.

Communication

During the infant's first years, your goal as a parent will be to plant the seeds that will help him eventually develop self-control, self-esteem and self-confidence as well as the barest beginnings of compliance.

To do this, begin by spending a lot of time talking to the baby. The human voice is very comforting to a child, and even though at first she won't understand very much of what you are saying, she will as time goes on. Eventually she will be able to take what you say seriously and incorporate your words into her understanding of society. How you communicate with an infant is very important. A child who has been comforted and talked to in a calm, reassuring manner from early infancy will feel okay about herself and is therefore more likely to be compliant and to get along easily with others. The things you say to your child become part of her internal speech and attitudes about herself. For this reason, I don't like to hear parents criticize their children harshly. A child who grows up saying to herself, "Boy, am I stupid," or "Wow, am I a jerk," or "How idiotic of me" probably heard someone say these things to her at an early age.

A child can benefit from calm, rational comments about right behavior and wrong behavior, even though at twelve to eighteen months she won't yet know the difference. It is important to communicate these concepts to her now, because you are laying the groundwork for the development of judgment and empathy later on. To do this, the parent can point out inappropriate behavior, not by yelling "no"—which may trigger a bad reaction and can become an irritating part of a child's vocabulary in the toddler years—but by telling the child calmly that what she is doing is not a good idea: "Jeremy is very angry that you took his pail away. Think how you would feel if someone took yours," or, "The radiator is very hot. If you touch the radiator, your hand will get burned and it will hurt a lot. I don't want your hand to get burned, so I don't want you to touch the radiator." These rational explanations and verbal exercises in sound judgment will be virtually incomprehensible to the small child, who is incapable of heeding good advice. But if such communication becomes part of that child's internal dialogue, the payoff may be enormous later when she is first learning to make her own good judgments.

REALISTIC EXPECTATIONS, PARENTAL GOALS AND TECHNIQUES FOR INFANTS

REALISTIC EXPECTATIONS

1. Between birth and three months, parents should have no discipline-related expectations.
2. Between three and six months, an infant can be distracted for very short periods.
3. Between six and twelve months, an infant may become mobile and may exhibit exaggerated clinging behavior.

4. Infants up to eighteen months cannot resist temptation.
5. Infants up to eighteen months cannot achieve reliable self-control.
6. Parents should not expect either compliance or obedience from infants. Imposing punishment during infancy is inappropriate and ineffective.

PARENTAL GOALS

1. Allow the infant to feel comfortable both with himself and with his environment.
2. Allow the infant to have an impact on his environment by being responsive to his demands.
3. Soften frustration for the infant.
4. Protect the infant from hazards.
5. Steer the infant in the direction of self-control, self-esteem and self-confidence.

TECHNIQUES

1. Anticipate problems before they occur.
2. Employ distraction.
3. Intervene when necessary.
4. Cajole the infant.
5. Use humor often.
6. Remove temptation.
7. Talk to the infant often.
8. Avoid criticism or sarcasm.
9. Help older infants identify their feelings.

COMMON PROBLEMS IN INFANCY

Scheduling

Scheduling a baby is a form of discipline. A mother imposes a schedule on a baby so that he can gradually learn to go for longer and longer periods without food, with the eventual goal that he be able to eat three or four meals a day, in keeping with social traditions. Disciplining a baby to a feeding schedule is also done for the sake of the parents and the family. As I mentioned earlier, I find it is always useful to ask yourself, "In whose interest am I doing this?" when making a discipline decision. Occasionally the action contemplated will be in the child's interest alone and not in the parent's or the family's. Sometimes the reverse will be true. In the best of all possible worlds, the two interests will merge. I think this is the case with feeding schedules. You have to help the child fit into the society in which he will grow up. And you have to give yourself a little room for other activities.

I think that by the age of three or four months, a baby is ready to be introduced to the idea of scheduling. Certainly, before that time, I would not frustrate a hungry infant. Not only is his digestive system too immature to go for very long without food, but he cannot yet be distracted from hunger.

As with other efforts to change a child's behavior, a gradual approach is desirable. According to pediatricians, breast-fed babies tend to eat more frequently than those who are bottle-fed. To suddenly impose a rigid mealtime schedule would be cruel and damaging to your baby. It would create excessive and very unsettling frustration that could disrupt your infant's growth and development.

Try to assess whether he needs to be fed each time he is fussy. Perhaps other activities will keep him occupied for a short period. This will help gradually increase the time span between feedings. Not all fussiness is due to hunger; you can usually tell which nursings are for a full feeding and which are for pacification. The scheduling of feeding times will become easier when solids are introduced.

Scheduling is an ongoing issue of self-discipline that begins in early infancy and continues, in a variety of forms, throughout childhood. Although your primary *interest* may be to alleviate your own frustration when the child's schedule interferes with yours, your primary *goal* should be to keep the infant's frustration to a minimum.

Spoiling

The question of spoiling first crops up in early infancy. Many parents feel that if they "give in" to an infant's cries, they will spoil the child for good. They complain that sometimes they can't put the child down for a minute—or they succumb to advice from others who tell them babies have to learn to entertain themselves.

With all due respect to the wisdom, judgment and experience of our elders, I don't think you can spoil a four-month-old baby. An infant needs you to be his arms and legs because he can't do very much for himself. Young babies are very social creatures. They don't like to be alone, and it's not a very good idea to force them to be alone just to teach them how to cope with it. Babies like to be carried around because they want to see things and want to know what is going on. They also want to be close to your body. These are important needs, and attending to them has nothing to do with spoiling.

Nothing will be gained by letting the baby cry simply to break him of his habit or of his need to be with you so much. If you carry him around and make him feel comfortable and secure and give him an opportunity to cling to his heart's content, my guess is that later on he will be much more able to venture out on his own. He isn't going to want to be held forever. At around nine or ten months, when he can first stand up and pull himself along the furniture and then walk, he might not even let you hold him when you want to.

Hoping that an infant will be able to entertain himself for any length of time is an expectation he can't live up to, but there are a few techniques you can try that will work for a few minutes when necessary. I know that it is very difficult to carry a baby while you are trying to shop or clean or pay bills. There are devices sold today that allow you to hold the baby next to you but keep your hands free; beyond that you might try putting the baby in an infant seat for two or three minutes and employing some tricks to keep him occupied. Stay in the room with the baby while he is in the seat; talk to him and look directly at him. Keep your eyes near his face and sing to him or kiss him or make faces so that he learns to associate enjoyable activities with sitting in the seat. See if he can become comfortable in the seat for short periods while watching you. After the three minutes are up, take the baby out of the infant seat and carry him around again. When you pick him up, talk to him while you're walking around. As I've said before, the human voice is very comforting to a baby. What you're trying to do is gradually accustom the infant to the little bit of frustration of not being in your arms. You can help the baby learn: "Yes, Mommy is still here. Even though I'm not in her arms, I'm still okay." This is a constructive form of discipline.

To worry about spoiling an infant by comforting him when he cries is needless. Expecting such a young child to be able to entertain himself for fifteen minutes or half an hour in a playpen or a stroller really is asking too much. Some placid babies may appear to be content in a playpen, but in general an infant's repertoire of self-entertaining activities is quite limited. What can he do? Look at a mobile, look at his fingers and toes, coo a little bit? If you put the baby in a playpen and the baby cries, pick him up. His crying isn't a habit you should try to break. Your baby can't be taught not to cry.

Giving an infant constant attention is hard work for parents and may seem awfully confining, but the stage is relatively short-lived and the payoff tremendous. Instead of a baby who feels miserable about himself, you'll have a comfortable and happy baby who feels quite terrific.

Screaming

Many parents are often baffled when infants are belligerent and have what appear to be uncontrollable screaming fits. One mother of an eight-month-old described such an episode this way: "If my daughter wants something, she screams bloody murder. She'll clench her fists and just let loose. Even if you take something away from her temporarily, like if I have to wipe a balloon off for her because she's dropped it, she'll just scream her head off."

Infants lack self-control. They react spontaneously to frustration and anxiety, and are incapable of listening to reason. Therefore, no matter how reasonable you've been, if you have to frustrate a baby, expect a fit in return. It isn't bad behavior—it's merely a normal outburst.

At eight months of age, a baby doesn't understand the concept of ownership. She has no idea that things belong to other people, and that when she wants something and reaches out for it she might not be able to have it. At this age, I would go along with that perception and attitude. If she drops a balloon and it gets dirty and you have to wipe it off, say to her, "I'm just cleaning it. I'll give it back to you in a minute."

An eight-month-old's screaming is normal, and isn't something to be alarmed about. Babies don't understand patience and have little, if any, tolerance for frustration. You will have to entertain your child a lot.

You may also find at about nine months that your baby will have a prolonged crying or screaming fit every time you put her down. This is quite normal. At this stage, many babies demonstrate an exaggerated separation anxiety and clinginess. Your baby will want to be around you, and she will worry when you walk away from her. Putting her in the playpen to get her out of the way, then, will not be met with joy, but you can teach her to have fun there by making it an interesting place to spend a moment or two. Play with her and introduce new toys in the playpen, and keep the time short. After ample orientation, she may be willing to entertain herself for a brief time.

Some parents become very anxious when their baby screams because they fear that allowing such behavior will teach her that such fits are acceptable. My advice is not to worry about that. When she is older, say three, and occasionally behaves like this, you will be better able to deal with it because by then she will have the beginnings of judgment. Also, as the infant acquires speech, her screaming will abate. Talking calmly to her while she is impatient will help her develop some control. It is not an immediate cause and effect, but over time, with a great deal of repetition, she will come to realize that a moment is a brief interval.

Sleep Problems

Many parents worry when their baby does not sleep through the night, or when they are unable to get their baby to fall asleep and wake up at civilized hours. First let me say that it is a myth that all infants should sleep until morning, and a hopeless expectation that older infants will promptly fall asleep at a designated bedtime. Second, I would like to emphasize that although some sleep problems may have psychological implications, many stem from physical causes. When a baby wakes up, parents should check first for some kind of physical discomfort. The infant may have gotten into an uncomfortable position or need help turning over. Hunger, teething or gas pains may be the source of the problem; so may a wet diaper or being too warm or too cold. A stuffed-up nose, a cough or a fever also frequently disrupt sleep. Sometimes a child will wake up simply because a pacifier has slipped out of his mouth.

When children do wake up and cry in the middle of the night, I do not believe that they should be left to "cry it out." Tears and whimpers should be ignored only if they subside quickly; screaming or wailing should never go unanswered. As I mentioned earlier, nothing is more distressing to an infant than to have his cry for attention ignored. And remember, the more available you are to your baby now, the more likely he will have a strong sense of security later.

Many parents encounter difficulties when the baby habitually falls asleep at the breast and is unable to fall asleep without it. This may become an undesirable dependency, especially since it prohibits anyone but the mother from putting the child to bed.

It's a very natural routine for a nursing baby to fall into. Infants awaken when they are hungry and fall asleep when they are satisfied. To break your child of this habit at four or five months, I suggest that you try to be alert to the signals he gives you just before he conks out. Some babies heave a big sigh and others roll their eyes just before they sleep. When you see the signs, remove the nipple from his mouth and lay the child down. He will probably become distressed. If so, pick him up, comfort him and give him the breast again if necessary. When he shows those telltale signs, lay him down once again and repeat the procedure. You will probably have to do this many times before the baby is able to fall asleep without the breast in his mouth, and it will require tremendous patience on your part. But in so doing, you will accustom your baby to crossing the threshold into sleep in a prone position, without the nipple in his mouth—thus encouraging in him a small measure of valuable independence.

Another common problem is the infant who has his days and nights mixed up. Most babies sleep at least twelve hours over a twenty-four-hour period. It is not unbroken sleep, of course, and some babies may need help to become oriented to the conventional day-and-night rhythm. To do this, you may have to manipulate your child's sleeping schedule. Let's say your child sleeps from 4:00 A.M. until noon, and you, of course, would prefer that he sleep from 10:00 P.M. to 6:00 A.M. One way to accomplish this is to clip about twenty minutes from his morning sleep so that gradually he falls asleep a bit earlier in the evening. After three or four days, wake him another twenty minutes earlier and so on until your goal is reached. Establishing a routine helps steer a baby into a sleep-wake cycle that is convenient for you and your family. Try to develop a bedtime ritual so that sleep at night becomes distinguished from daytime naps.

Even after you have established a good sleep-wake cycle, you may discover that your baby suddenly begins waking up several times during the night. This often happens with slightly older infants who have just learned how to stand or walk. Sometimes the sense of independence that comes with a new accomplishment can be frightening. You should quietly calm the child. Talk in soothing tones, keep the area dimly lighted and reassure him with some pats on the back. When the novelty of the accomplishment wears off, the untimely waking will abate.

As your infant approaches toddlerhood, you may find that his new-found independence creates other problems. For example, an older infant will often decide he no longer wants to sleep in a crib. Some parents fight needlessly with their children, insisting that they continue to sleep there; others actually put a net over the crib to keep the child from climbing out. My feeling is that you should heed your child's messages and not make him a prisoner. It's very unsettling to be trapped that way. Older infants have a strong urge to explore, and they need room to grow. Why not allow your child to "camp out"? Try letting him sleep in a sleeping bag on the floor in his room. Or perhaps you could put the mattress from his crib on the floor, placing some cushions around it so he won't be injured if he rolls off. If you discover that he prefers these or other alternative sleeping arrangements, ask him if he would like the crib removed from his room. If he's comfortable with that idea, then do so—you'll be making the inevitable transition from a crib to a bed easier for both of you later on.

Temper Tantrums

When a child's frustration leads to anger, the child may have a fit of bad temper—what we call a tantrum. A tantrum doesn't mean that the child is bad. All babies want to get their way—the sooner the better!

Often parents become very alarmed at the thought of their baby having a bad temper. Either they think there is something wrong with the child, or else they find it distasteful. Unnerved by what they perceive as unattractive behavior, they believe that if they deal with the child in a particular way, they will be able to stamp out these reactions and get him to behave in a polite, pleasant fashion.

Such endeavors will be fruitless. A temper tantrum is a natural consequence of a child not having what he wants at the moment. Children don't have words at six or eight or ten months to say to you, "Darn it! I really wanted that," or "Why can't I have that?" or "It's not fair!"—expressions you will hear plenty of later on. At this age the only thing the child can do is scowl, scream or throw a tantrum to communicate his emotions. Without adequate speech, feelings of frustration and anger are conveyed directly through such outbursts.

Disciplining a child in relation to the way he expresses his feelings is probably one of the most important tasks parents face. Children need to be taught to recognize their feelings and to identify them properly at given times. The outward expression of a feeling is the first step in a child's becoming aware of his emotions. Next comes education, the real meaning of discipline: Once a child knows what his feelings are, then he must learn alternative ways to show them. Anger is an especially important emotion for children to learn about.

As a parent, you should try to resist the temptation to label angry feelings as ugly or bad. You may be able to stifle the outward expression of anger, but you will never be able to make the anger itself go away. Instead, the child may turn the anger inward with potentially harmful consequences to himself. By attempting to discipline the child not to have a temper tantrum, what you are really saying to him is: "Don't show me your feelings."

Of course, your baby is still too young to get a complete education in this emotion. With older infants, I suggest that you use distraction techniques very liberally and begin to say things like "You are very annoyed because you couldn't have that." Later, your child will incorporate a vocabulary that includes "angry," "furious," "irritated," "perturbed" and other words to express anger. This provides an outlet for feelings and may lessen behavioral outbursts and permit greater self-control. (For a fuller discussion of how to control temper tantrums in older children, see the chapter on toddlers.)

Protecting a Child from Hazardous Play

Imagine this scenario: An eleven-month-old boy becomes fascinated by the wood stove in the family room. To warn him away, the boy's father tells him "No!" quite sharply several times. The boy still tries to touch the wood stove. The father gets up, drags the boy back and slaps his hand. "No!" he yells again. Incredibly, the boy turns and looks at the wood stove and heads right for it. The frustrated father loses his temper and gives the boy a hard smack. He does it for the boy's own good—for his safety—right?

Wrong. Hitting an eleven-month-old child is not going to stop him from trying to touch a wood stove. As long as the temptation is there, and until the child has better judgment, he is going to yield to his desire.

Telling the child "No!" won't work either. I'm against using the word "no" without an explanation because it can actually stimulate the child to proceed further with the action, and because the word will come back to haunt you when it becomes entrenched in the child's vocabulary around the age of two. Instead, use whole sentences such as "That's hot and very dangerous. If you touch it, you will get burned."

Even though I like parents to give children full explanations, I don't want to mislead you into thinking they will achieve any immediate results. Until the child actually catches on to the idea that the stove gives off heat, the verbal instruction alone won't mean very much to him. Yet I do think you should say it, simply to accustom the child to attending to your words, so that later on when he is able to comprehend warnings and advice, he will be more likely to heed them.

By saying that a child won't really understand your warning, I do not mean to suggest that you let him go off and experiment with a hot wood stove. Children do have terrible accidents—pulling down a pot of scalding water from the stove, for example—and you have to protect them from such disasters. The only recourse is to intervene. Since you can't remove the wood stove from the room, you have to remove the child from the wood stove. If possible, try to "baby-proof" your home so that the child can't get hurt. If that is not feasible, then you will simply have to run over to the child each time he gets near a dangerous object and take him away from it. The child will probably turn this activity into a game, running as close as he dares and then waiting for you to run over and get him. It's a lot of hard work always to be alert to where the child is, but you really don't have much choice.

Before it turns into a game, however, I suggest you try distracting the child so that his running over to a dangerous object doesn't become a contest for both of you. The first time you see the child nearing any forbidden object or territory, very quietly get his attention without mentioning the prohibited object, and say, "Oh, look what I have here!" Pick him up and introduce him to a different activity.

Expecting an eleven-month-old to control his initial impulses to touch something and to tolerate the frustration of being forbidden to touch it is unrealistic. When a child that age sees a radiator, he wants to feel it. He doesn't know it's going to burn him. And even if he does burn himself on one particular radiator, that doesn't necessarily mean he's going to know that the next radiator will burn him, too. Sitting back and saying "no" to a child as he marches forward to the radiator will not only be ineffective, but will also lead to tremendous frustration for you because you are not being obeyed. The child is incapable of obeying you at this age. He doesn't have the self-control necessary for obedience.

Biting, Hitting and Hair Pulling

Around the age of thirteen or fourteen months, children seem to acquire a kind of sadistic streak. It's fairly common for them at this age to experiment with biting, hitting and hair pulling. A little bit of this behavior resurfaces around twenty months, when some children try punching, shoving and pinching. Observation seems to indicate that this is probably a developmental phase. However, that doesn't mean that it should go unnoticed.

If your child is a biter, hitter or hair puller, you will have to supervise her carefully when she is with other children. The minute you see her start to pull another child's hair, you must intervene and remove her hands from the other child. Walk your daughter away, and in a firm but not too distraught voice, say to her that hair pulling hurts other people. Tell her you don't like it when she pulls hair and that you and she will have to leave the play area for five minutes. It may not be terribly effective, but it does remove her from the situation.

A far more effective approach will be possible when she pulls *your* hair or bites you. The technique I suggest is that you immediately— without any hesitation at all—and quite harshly and with some anger, bend down and look her straight in the eye and say, "That hurt me. I don't want you to hurt me. Now I'm going into the other room for a minute, and you just stay here." Then turn around and walk away from her. She should have a strong reaction to that. She will probably try to trail after you. If your spouse or someone else is present, ask that person to stop her from coming after you by saying, "Mom's inside. She'll be back in a moment. But you hurt her, so she had to leave you for a few minutes."

Don't try to have a big discussion about it. It won't mean anything to her. Likewise, don't run over and make up to her and say everything will be all right. She will probably cry. Let her have her cry. Let her worry. The point of this exercise is to make her realize that when she bites or pulls hair she risks your anger, and your absence. Worrying about that should stop her.

I have heard people advise parents to bite their children back or hit them or pull their hair, presumably to demonstrate that it hurts. Please don't do that! A young child will not be able to make the connection between how she feels when you bite or hit her and how it feels to you when she is the perpetrator. Such empathy requires a greater degree of maturity than your baby has right now. Hurting her back is no way to stop her experimental, albeit painful, behavior.

Getting Into Things

Recently a mother called to tell me her eighteen-month-old son was getting into things. She said her apartment was about as child-proof as it could be, but that her son's primary passion was constantly opening the refrigerator to take out what he wanted. If he decided he wanted apple juice, he'd open the fridge and get the bottle. Or he'd take out a couple of eggs and put them on the couch. He knew that his mother didn't want him to do this, so he tried to do it when she was occupied with something else, such as washing the dishes or getting ready to go out. She'd tried to distract him with blocks and other toys. It had worked a couple of times, but wasn't working any more. She ended her call by saying that she thought she had a real "discipline" problem on her hands.

It was very interesting to me that she referred to this as a matter of discipline, but what was really happening had more to do with her son's curiosity and with his developing ability to get what he wanted for himself. If you think about it, it's perfectly normal to open the refrigerator and look inside. Older children do that; adults do that. When we want a snack we often open the fridge and stand there for a minute, thinking, "Let's see what's in here." For an eighteen-month-old boy, it's even more intriguing than it is for an adult, because he doesn't have our twenty-five or thirty years of experience opening refrigerators; he has only a few months. While I don't think a refrigerator is a toy, I do think a child needs an opportunity to satisfy his curiosity. Once that's accomplished, you may rest assured that he will become bored with his explorations. He won't open refrigerators forever.

If you want to distract a small child from exploring forbidden territory, you might try offering him something that closely relates to the object that excites him so. If your son wants apple juice and is opening the fridge to get at it, blocks may not be the appropriate distraction, whereas a drink of juice at the table or some cheese might be more successful.

Distraction won't always work, however. His curiosity is normal, and as a parent, you certainly don't want to "discipline" your child's curiosity away.

One of life's problems is that we have to put our children in environments that contain things that aren't meant for them and occasionally aren't safe for them. There is no easy way around having to supervise your child constantly. Even if you have child-proofed your home, you still can't prevent a curious child from wanting to climb up on a counter and look in the cupboard, or climbing onto the couch to touch the stereo. To the extent that you can, allow a child to explore and satisfy his curiosity—but with you in attendance.

Remember, a child's exploration of forbidden territory is partially born of fascination. It is also an effort toward greater independence on his part. The boy opening the refrigerator wanted to be able to help himself to a snack. Some parents designate the bottom shelf for items that the child may help himself to freely. If a child is ready for such responsibility, a solution like this one might cut down on the parents' constantly having to thwart his efforts.

Disobedience?

Expecting obedience or compliance from an infant is foolhardy at best. Even fifteen- and eighteen-month-olds lack the kind of physical maturity and self-control that would make obedience possible. Many of a fifteen-month-old's activities, for example, involve what we call "gross motor coordination"—activities such as climbing, walking up and down steps, swinging on things and going up the ladder to the slide. Unless your child is a very mellow, laid-back sort of fifteen-month-old, it's fruitless to hope that he will climb gracefully onto a changing table and lie still for a diaper change, or comply by standing still when you are dressing him. It's really not a matter of obedience; rather, it's a factor of the child's developing skills, and of your expectations aligning with this development.

Many parents have asked me: "How do I get my child to sit still long enough to eat?" Some kids eat standing; some eat on the run, swooping down like birds after prey and flying onward. This is just the way kids are, and expecting a child to sit still for dinner is probably just as unrealistic at this age as expecting him to lie still for a diaper change.

So how do you get the diaper changed or the child dressed? You have to involve him in something else while you get the job done. Give him something to hold while you change him or put on his pants. As you attempt to qualify for the *Guinness Book of World Records* for the quickest diaper change in the country, hand the child a toy and say to him, "Hang on to this for a second." Speed and distraction are what you should aim for at this age—not obedience or cooperation.

Tolerating your child's developmental needs and capabilities may, on occasion, become a source of conflict. You imagine that others, seeing your child act willful and "disobedient," are making cracks about your inability to be "in charge" or to "control" your child. As a parent, you will have to steel yourself against the petty looks and comments some people who were raised with a different philosophy of child rearing will make when you treat your child in a manner you think right. There isn't anything you can do about this. I understand that it might make you very uncomfortable, but that discomfort isn't as important as allowing your child to climb a set of stairs a dozen times or stop every ten feet along the sidewalk on an outing. Your child needs an opportunity to explore and to practice large motor skills such as climbing, and she should have the chance to do it. It's boring for you, but she's learning coordination, balance and judgment.

I would like to applaud a couple I noticed in a restaurant the other day who were there with their child. The girl was about fourteen-months old, at an age when she just wasn't able to sit still in a restaurant long enough to eat a meal. Between each course, one of the parents got up and took the child for a walk. The child walked cheerfully up the stairs and down the stairs and called out sounds of delight. The couple was smart. They came early, when there weren't too many other people in the restaurant, and they took turns keeping the child active but out of mischief. It meant eating only a few nibbles here and there, and it certainly wasn't what you would call a relaxed, gracious meal. And the parents had to ignore some raised eyebrows. But they had their priorities straight. Instead of expecting cooperation and obedience from a child who couldn't possibly give it to them in that situation, they allowed her to be a fourteen-month-old child. Proper planning is essential. If you want to enjoy a meal out, don't take the baby along. If you decide to take your child, see it as an opportunity for her to become accustomed to restaurants. It is practice for the future. Bring along some of her favorite foods. Let her taste your dishes. Take turns occupying her. Remember, her developmental needs may not be in sync with your needs for recreation and relaxation. And she is too young to be considerate of your wishes.

Throwing Food

A sixteen-month-old often thinks food is something to play with. The mess can be awful. Mealtimes become chaotic. You give your child something to eat. He throws it on the floor. You're supposed to pick it up. Or else he digs in with his hands, squishes it and smears it all over himself. When your parents come to visit, they're horrified. They tell you to spoon-feed your son and not allow him to make these kinds of messes.

It's very natural for a young child to experiment with food. Although we consider food something to be eaten, a child can't put it into such a clear-cut category. For an infant, it may be yummy to eat, but it's also yummy to play with. It's fun to throw because it makes a good sound and it's fun to squish, and almost certainly playing with food will get a rise out of your parents.

Playing with food at this age has to be expected. Once you know that, controlling your temper when it happens may be easier. Parents often find it very hard to tolerate the mess of feeding an infant. As adults, we have learned to be neat and organized. We respect cleanliness, and we aren't comfortable with messes. Therefore, we find it very difficult to tolerate impulsive, self-centered, wasteful behavior in others—especially in our own children. The desire and respect for orderliness operates at some deeper level of consciousness that may make us feel uncomfortable when we watch our children eat.

Of course, you want to teach your child that he shouldn't play with food. But you aren't going to be successful immediately. This lesson must be learned gradually, in stages. In the beginning, there will have to be some give and take between you and your child. You can let him experiment with squishing a banana for a time, but once it becomes clear that he's interested merely in playing with it and no longer in eating it, say to him, "I think you've squished the banana long enough. I don't think you are hungry anymore." Then take the child out of the high chair and go on to the next activity, which will probably be over to the sink to wash his face and hands.

Children this age are just learning how to throw, and they enjoy the "scientific experiment"—watching the trajectory and seeing just how far they can hurl something. Food is often the most ready object at hand, and an infant doesn't give much thought to what kind of mess the object will make. Nor does he much care that he is wasting food. These concepts are really lost on an infant, who is more interested in the game of throwing.

Some children will engage you in another kind of game. They throw the food on the floor and then expect you to pick it up. Although this behavior may seem maddening, it's part of learning about letting go of something and having it come back, and is symbolic of the larger emotional issue about people going away and coming back. Resist the impulse to stop your child from playing this game. It's actually quite valuable practice for his gradual emotional and physical separation from you.

Once you have accustomed yourself to all the mess of infant feeding, then you'll have to decide what to do when, for example, Aunt Mary comes to visit and finds such behavior nearly intolerable. Child-rearing theories change and evolve; we now feed our infants quite differently from the way we ourselves were fed as babies. Remember when your mother spoon-fed your baby brother, wiping his face and chin after every mouthful? Many of us now believe that this may not be the best way to teach a child to be independent and self-reliant about eating, and that spoon-feeding an older infant or a toddler can become intrusive. But as far as Aunt Mary is concerned, all that mess indicates to her that you've lost control over your child, or that you're "spoiling" him.

The answer I have for this dilemma can be applied to many situations in which your philosophy of child rearing conflicts with that of others. You have to know in your heart that it is you who must live with the consequences of your child rearing decisions—not your friends, relatives or neighbors. Once incorporated into your own thinking, this attitude has to be conveyed to any outsider—whether it's the bus driver who doesn't like the way you let your child drop the token into the slot, your aunt who is critical of the way you feed your child, or the checkout clerk who thinks you don't have your child in control at the supermarket. If you think what you're doing is right, don't be swayed by anybody's raised eyebrows.

TODDLERS:
NEGOTIATING THE ENVIRONMENT

Even parents who were fairly relaxed about matters of discipline when their children were younger will suddenly find that, between the ages of eighteen months to three years, their children are becoming much more mobile and verbal. They seem to be enormously self-centered and surprisingly resistant to your requests or demands. On some days they will have hair-trigger tempers or inexhaustible reserves of guile and cunning. On other days, power struggles will dominate your relationship with these mystifying rebels. The toddler age has been called "the terrific twos," and for most children it is a joyous period of growth and development, but it has also been dubbed "the terrible twos" by parents who have reason to know. Not surprisingly, many parents first face the issue of discipline at this difficult age.

What governs a two-year-old? Perhaps the most useful piece of information I can give the parents of a toddler is that a child between the ages of eighteen months and three years does not have an inner sense of what is right and what is wrong. The child's sense of values or morality is perhaps slightly better developed than it was a few months ago, but it is

still not much to write home about. What's good and what's bad seldom
crosses a toddler's mind, except when your approval or disapproval is
made clear. A much more engaging issue for a two-year-old is what's
pleasurable and what's not. Or, more to the point: What do I want and
what do I not want?

To assume that your toddler knows right from wrong or good from bad
is almost certain to get you into trouble if you try to discipline him on
that basis. How often has a parent said to a toddler, "I told you a million
times. Don't do that. You'll break it"? Such a speech means little or
nothing to the child, however, because every time he sees that interesting piece of pottery, it's still interesting, and the urge to grab it, look at it,
play with it, make an echo sound in it or stick his hand inside it and feel
around is too strong: It's what he *wants* to do. What he *ought* to do is
not the issue with him. The fact that Mom had a fit last time he touched
it—even if the child happens to remember this, which is by no means
certain—cannot begin to overwhelm his urge to do it. Warnings from
Mom cannot relate to any inner sense of right and wrong, because such
a sense doesn't exist to help the child overcome the temptation.

Many a parent has said to me, "When I tell my child not to do
something, I can see this sly little grin creep over her face, and then she
goes right ahead and does it. Doesn't that mean that she knows the
difference between right and wrong, and she's just being mischievous?"

The answer is, not really! It's not a question of internal morality.
Rather, it's a question of what *you*, the authority figure, will permit and
not permit. To a large extent, you are a policeman to the child. In her
mind, an act is wrong only if Mom or Dad doesn't allow it. If, for
instance, you were to go into another room, the child would feel no
compunction about doing the thing you asked her not to do. If she
doesn't get caught, what's the problem? The sly grin, then, is a tease.
But at this age, the child feels no guilt. She has no ability to make
judgments. To do that would require a sense of morality, memory and
self-control—none of which the toddler possesses in reliable amounts
yet.

The task of putting your expectations in line with your child's mental,
social and emotional capabilities is often confusing at this stage because,
compared to six months ago, your child will appear to be very clever and
smart. It is easy for a parent to begin to think that the child is deliberately defying him, or that without some strenuous form of punishment,
the child will soon be out of control or spoiled. As the child develops
and is able to make his wants known verbally and physically, some fairly

intense power struggles with his parents become likely. Stubbornness and temper tantrums may ensue. This unattractive behavior develops not because the child feels bad that his parents don't want him to have something, but because he feels angry that he wants it and Mom or Dad won't let him have it.

Occasionally a two-year-old may show some beginnings of empathy and caring about another person's feelings. For instance, you will sometimes see a toddler go over to comfort Mom if she is crying. But even this suggestion of empathy may be quite self-centered. The child wants to make Mom better fast, because seeing Mom as a vulnerable person is scary. If Mom is in trouble, who is going to take care of me? the child is thinking. Although there is probably some natural sadness at seeing another person cry, the overriding goal is to get Mom into better shape quickly.

This self-centeredness is a natural outgrowth of one of the toddler's major concerns: What is me and what is mine? Toddlers are very much governed by the discovery of self. This is why most toddlers are incapable of sharing, for example. When a toddler is asked to share, he fears that if the object is not actually in his own hands, it no longer belongs to him. This may seem wildly irrational, but to a toddler, what's his is what he can get his hands on. Even more threatening is when something is taken away from him. He feels as though a piece of him—an integral piece—is being torn from him. You'll often see a toddler defending to the death, so to speak, some small object or toy that belongs to him. You'll also see, however, a toddler having a fit over something that doesn't belong to him, but that he momentarily has in his possession. Let's say a toddler happens to notice a toy across the room that another child is walking toward, and he suddenly makes a beeline for it and snatches it up before anyone else can. It isn't greed that governs his behavior. It's that the child is saying to himself, "I like that toy. It's mine." The toy becomes part of the child's self-system, and if you try to take it away from him, you will be met with outrage, screaming and possibly a temper tantrum.

A toddler has very poor judgment. For example, you've told your child many times not to run into the street after the ball. Come and get me, you've said, and I'll go get the ball. Or you've told the child not to run across the street to Rachel's house by himself, but to come get you and you will take him across. You have explained that a car might come along and that it would be dangerous. You've explained this many times. And then one day, the child runs into the street without even thinking. How can he *do* that? you ask yourself. The answer is quite simple. He doesn't for one minute understand his mortality. A two-year-old child can't possibly conceive of a car doing him any harm; the only thing he has in his mind is getting to the other side of the street. His reasoning goes like this: "Oh, there's my friend. I'm going to cross the street." Mortality just isn't part of his thinking yet.

There are exceptions. Some children are very timid and fearful. They wouldn't dream of crossing the street without Mom or climbing onto a countertop. But a parent shouldn't be deceived into thinking this timidity is an example of good judgment.

Climbing up onto a countertop to reach for something is quite natural. A child learns that if she climbs onto a chair, this will get her onto the counter, which in turn gets her onto a shelf. Hey, that's great, thinks the child. What's wrong with that? It's an accomplishment, a feat. Of course, you know there are probably twenty-seven things wrong with it—she might hurt herself getting up or down, or break something that belongs to you—but to the child, this is just as terrific an experience as sitting on the floor in the kitchen, beating some eggs into the linoleum and mixing cereal into the mess in an earnest effort to put breakfast together for you.

Does this mean that you should just smile and applaud these "accomplishments"? Of course not. As I urged you to do in the infant years, you will have to supervise, intervene and distract to protect your child from harm and to protect your property from his curious probings. I think you can also now begin to explain to your child why he shouldn't climb onto the countertop or run into the street. As in the previous stage of development, these rational explanations are likely to go unheeded, but you should get into the habit of providing them so that the child will get into the habit of hearing and learning to attend to them. It's a good investment for the future.

For example, you find your toddler on the top shelf of your closet. Rather than yanking the child out and possibly precipitating a big fight, say to him, "I told you not to climb up there. It's very dangerous. Is there something that you wanted up there?" Perhaps there was a box of shoes or scarves the child had his eye on. "Did you want that box of shoes?" you might say. "Here, Mommy will get it for you." Instead of dealing with the incident as an infraction, try to understand the child's ambition. If what he wants is something you're not worried about his damaging, why not give it to him? It's not spoiling a child to give him what he was after. He wanted a box of shoes and had the ambition and initiative to go get it himself.

Another child may take it upon himself to explore the closet simply because it feels good to be up high, to be rummaging around in all those clothes, with all those interesting smells, and touching all the things in there. Obviously you can't allow a child to be alone on a high shelf, but rather than snatching him off and punishing him, think about giving him an opportunity to explore—since exploration seems to be very much on his mind. A drawer full of clothes from your bureau, for example, might easily satisfy him.

As the parent of a toddler, you will be called upon to be very watchful. Offering suitable alternative activities is essential, too, and about 90 percent of discipline during this stage of development consists of these tactics. However, you can begin to impose, to a limited extent, some mild, humane and logically related punishments so that the child can get the message that there are unpleasant consequences when he does undesirable things. This probably won't work right away, but it's excellent practice for both you and your child. And as the following example illustrates, it can also give you both a moment of relief: If you say to a child who is misbehaving, "Sit in that chair and stay there for a minute," you've removed the child from the situation so that he is not able to continue, and you get a chance to regain your composure.

If your child is throwing blocks, a logically related punishment is to put the blocks away. Tell your child that they will not be available again until some specified time—not a very long time, just long enough to make the point: "You may not play with the blocks anymore for now. After dinner you may have them back." Of course, you'll have to put up with complaints, whines and cries. But so long as you are matter-of-fact and consistent, children do get the message and eventually relent. Don't escalate the punishment when your child had a reaction to the original one. Just stick to your decision (unless, of course, new evidence enters into the situation that may warrant a reversal of your judgment).

Another very big issue with toddlers is negativism. This leads to many arguments and power struggles. One is that parents are inclined to think logically, while toddlers are governed blissfully by their emotions. For instance, a parent pleads, "But you love peaches and we don't have any purple ice cream," while the determined toddler tearfully shrieks, "No, no, no. I don't want peaches. I hate peaches!"

It is essential to remember that even when you try to be conciliatory, a less-than-logical child can bring you to the utmost level of frustration. Toddlers may decline even their most coveted item at times. The drive to say "no" can overpower other desires. It is so very important for them to declare themselves separate from you that they may pick a fight just to show that they are different. In a toddler's mind, agreeing with you means that he is indistinguishable from you. Since becoming a separate person is a toddler's major goal, his need to establish boundaries is often felt with great urgency. This desire frequently results in what appear to be totally ridiculous tugs-of-war. More than ice cream or peaches is involved. The adamant little tot is fighting hard to solidify a personal sense of Self. Selfhood sometimes requires great sacrifice and often precludes cooperation. Discipline at this age means helping your child to attain a measure of autonomy.

REALISTIC EXPECTATIONS, PARENTAL GOALS AND TECHNIQUES FOR TODDLERS

REALISTIC EXPECTATIONS

1. The child does not yet have an inner sense of right and wrong.
2. The child probably cannot overcome temptation.
3. The child is quite self-centered. Only the barest beginnings of empathy are shown.
4. The child has poor judgment.
5. The child may be very negative.

PARENTAL GOALS

1. Help your child attain a measure of autonomy.
2. Protect your child from hazardous play or exploration.
3. Help your child attend to rational explanations—but just for practice (the child cannot yet fully understand them).
4. Help your child understand that there may be consequences to his actions.

TECHNIQUES

1. Intervene.
2. Supervise.
3. Distract.

4. Give the child advance notice.
5. Pick your battles.
6. Give rational explanations when appropriate.
7. Allow and encourage safe exploration.
8. Offer substitute activities.
9. Begin to impose some mild, humane and logically related punishments.
10. Thank the child for cooperating.

COMMON PROBLEMS IN TODDLERHOOD

Power Struggles

Struggles with children are unavoidable. Two-year-olds tend to be negative, but even older children have different points of view from yours, and you will have arguments with them. Between any two people, it is likely that on more than one occasion there will be conflicts. In the case of a parent and a toddler, it just so happens that you are bigger and stronger and smarter and older. You have a lot of authority and she doesn't have much, nor should she. Your judgment is better than hers. Nevertheless, she's going to want to say "no" to a lot of your requests and she's going to want to have her own way.

If you threaten her and hit her every time you have a power struggle, I can tell you that for the next year that's all you'll be doing, because this is the age when children say "no" to everything. It will be a horrible time for both of you. To avoid it, you need a series of different approaches to defuse these conflicts.

First, if the issue doesn't matter a whole lot, just drop it. You don't have to win every fight. I know that sometimes parents feel that they had better win or the child will get the idea that she can always overpower them. But that's not true. As children develop, they become a little more sensible; they develop some logic and they have a more reasonable outlook on life. They can resist temptation better and they can tolerate frustration more easily. Power struggles with them will lessen of their own accord, and you will not have lost any of your authority in the process by giving in when it doesn't matter very much.

On some occasions you may be able to negotiate a compromise. If your child wants to wear your high heels instead of her sneakers, for example, you might dissuade her with the promise of a reward. "I'll tell you what," you might say to her. "Put your sneakers on now. I'll put these high heels in a bag. See this bag? And I'll carry it out to the car. And when you get to Grandma's you can put on the high heels there and show them to her."

At other times you will have to distract your child by talking about something entirely different. And while you are talking to distract her, you will be walking her through the activity that you had in mind for her. For example, rather than saying to a child, "Put your sweater on now. I want you to wear this sweater," you'd be better off reminding the child of the last time you both went to Grandma's, when that little dog walked by you on the sidewalk... meanwhile, you are putting the child's arm into the sweater and walking her out the door.

One of the most frustrating situations for the parent of a toddler is when you have to get out the door, the child has to have her sneakers on, and you can't distract her successfully. You are unable to find a reward that will appease her and you can't talk her through the activity. In this case, you may have to overpower her physically and put the sneakers on, or you will have to carry her to the car without the sneakers, put her in the car seat and fasten the seat belt. She will scream, and it will be unpleasant, and it will probably happen on more than one occasion.

But try to avoid threatening and spanking. Power struggles are seldom lessened by laying on additional punishments. The fact that you have won the battle and that the child is in the car is, to the child, punishment enough. Why add insult to injury?

Picking Your Battles

Toddlers are terrifically active and often into everything. They will go to a bookcase and toss all the books around just so they can find the one they want. You'll ask them to help you put the books back, and the answer will be "no." Perhaps you'll start yelling. Perhaps you'll feel yourself becoming enraged. You try to be consistent, but you can't always. You feel that you're losing it. You don't want to spend your days yelling or saying "no" all the time, but you just don't know how much intervention is appropriate.

The trick is to know where to draw the line. Many of the activities your toddler is engaged in are typical of his age. In some instances, you can allow his normal behavior to play itself out; in other instances, intervention will be called for. Knowing when to intervene is often very difficult. No two incidents are ever exactly the same, and sometimes one infraction seems compounded by another. Any given issue can become quite complicated.

However, I urge you to pick only those battles that are worth fighting. If you don't, you may find that you're fighting all day with your child about one thing and another. It doesn't make any sense to do that, for a variety of reasons. Fighting all day with your child impairs your ability to form an intimate relationship with him, making it nearly impossible to spend calm rational time together so that other aspects of your relationship can develop; and it fosters the likelihood that you will, at some point in the day, lose your temper, which isn't desirable.

The rage that the child triggers in you is not at all unusual. Often it will seem as if the child is purposely trying to get your goat. Some of the time he may be, but not always. For example, you're trying to get him dressed and out of the house to meet a deadline. While you're frantically helping everyone else get ready, you discover that he's just lolling around and not paying any attention to you. You're filled with rage because you think he's deliberately defying you.

Although your feelings of rage are real, they may not be entirely appropriate in this instance. A child's sense of time is quite different from an adult's. He imagines that he can take all the time he wants and still be out by nine o'clock. This makes no sense to you, of course. You can see clearly that if you don't all start now, there is no possible way to be out of the house by nine. But that doesn't mean anything to the child. It's hard to blame a child for this deficiency in his logic. And you can't impose it on him simply by telling him. Instead, you have to help him be ready when you want him to be. This requires patience, guidance and a structure he can relate to.

You might try, for example, giving the child a clock and pointing out where the minute hand will be in five minutes, and suggesting that he put on one article of clothing in that time. Later, if he is successful, you can give him another five-minute time frame in which to put on something else. In this way, you will be helping the child by giving him more specific instructions, a structure that might even turn the chore into a game. Fighting over this issue, however, will almost certainly be futile, since the child is incapable of understanding your needs. This is what I mean by picking your battles.

Suppose your child is throwing books around and refuses to pick them up. Rather than let yourself become angry at this defiant and unattractive behavior, think for a minute and try to find some *leverage*. After he has tossed the books around and has finally picked out the one he wants you to read to him, take the book and place it very nicely in the chair where you will be sitting. After you have done that, say to him, "Okay, before we read this book, let's put these other books back so we'll know where to find them next time." If he is looking forward to having you read the book he's just chosen he might be more inclined to go along with putting back the ones he tossed out, because there is a goal at the end—you will read him a story.

Be careful, however, not to introduce putting the books away as a chore. Don't even make a verbal command out of it, because if you do, you can be sure he will then defy you. Instead, walk over to the books, invite him to join you, and when he gets there, turn it into a game. Say to him, "You take the tall ones and I'll take the short ones." Make the work pleasurable. If you don't actually label the work as a chore, the child is less likely to regard the activity as such, and less likely to rebel against it. Once you tell him you are assigning him something to do, it becomes a red flag that is almost certain to stimulate his rebelliousness.

In order to pick your battles wisely, sit down at night and make a list of all the little battles you and your toddler got into during the day. Select from this list the conflicts you think are absolutely necessary for one reason or another, but be sure to pick issues in which you have a bit of leverage. If you select those and are able to let some of the other conflicts go, you will shortly find that you are more on top of the situation and less likely to be overcome by rage.

When you do lose your temper, you may find yourself screaming at your child. In turn, you may discover that your child screams back at you. Two issues are involved when you are trying to resolve conflicts with toddlers. The first is to try to get a better grip on your own frustration and anger so that you do not constantly scream at your child. The second is to try to break the toddler of the habit of screaming at you. To some extent, a toddler's yelling is his way of coping with his own rage and frustration, which, as we have seen earlier, is quite common at this age. Some of the screaming, however, may be imitative. Parents who yell at their children or who bark out one-word commands can expect to see a lot of their own behavior imitated by their toddlers. It is for this reason that I urge parents not to resort to constant use of the word *no* when dealing with their young children.

The best way to get your child to stop yelling at you is to stop yelling at him. If he does yell at you (it may now be a habit and difficult to break), say to him, "Do you realize you are yelling at me right now? I don't like to be yelled at." Yelling back at him will not help, nor will hitting him. Most likely, he will begin hitting you back, and then you'll really find yourself in a difficult situation.

When you are enraged and feel on the verge of losing control, walk out of the room and count to ten. Decide if this is an emergency situation. Does he need to be in bed right now, for example, and is he resisting you? If that is the case and he is fighting you off by yelling or screaming "No, I won't go to bed," take a minute to think about what you need to do and how you can best accomplish it. You may have to overpower him, to pick him up and put him, wailing, into the bed. It won't be pleasant, but it is far better than screaming at him or hitting him.

If the situation isn't an emergency, just say to yourself, "The heck with it." Walk out of the room for five minutes with the intention of coming back to try again later. Perhaps by then tempers will have cooled off, and you may have an easier time of it. Often parents feel that when toddlers resist them, their authority is being challenged. They worry that the two-year-old is poking fun at them, and that their parental control will be lost forever. Rest assured that this is not the case. On the contrary, demonstating self-control in tense situations rather than losing your composure will enhance your authority in the child's eyes.

Running You Ragged

Raising a two-year-old can be a very trying experience. You may feel that just trying to keep up with him and to keep your sanity runs you ragged. However, what you are going through is not that unusual. You may think you are unique and that all your friends are looking askance at you, but I assure you that thousands of parents—hundreds of thousands of parents with two-year-olds—are going through exactly the same thing. Perhaps not all the time, but often.

The first thing you must realize is that you are not going to change your child, at least not right now. He is going to be this kind of person for a while. He may change in a year or two, but if he is an active child, he is going to retain some of his present traits, because he is who he is, at least for now.

There are some techniques I would advise you to try to make life a bit easier for the both of you. The first is *anticipation*. Let's say you have stopped by to look at the parakeets in the pet section of the department store and you know your son, like most children his age, is not going to want to leave just because you have something else to do. Your goal, then, should be to think up a way to get him to move without stirring up a big fight. Rather than saying, "Okay, it's time to leave now," invent a means to make that transition smoother.

One idea is to *distract* him by offering him something else equally interesting to look at. You have to go to the hardware department. Fine. Say to your toddler, "Hey, remember those pliers of Dad's that you wanted to use the other day? How would you like it if we went over to the hardware department and bought you your very own pair? You can look at all the pliers and pick out the ones you want." Chances are, there will always be something in a hardware or other store attractive enough to your child to distract his attention from the parakeets. The important point is not to mention that it's the end of the parakeet time. Children don't like to have things come to an end. Better to ignore the fact that one activity is ending and immediately focus instead on the fun of the activity about to come up.

Now, let's say you are in a situation where you can't offer the child another activity immediately. There is no hardware store to go to, but you do have to move on to other things. You might say to your son, "Okay, we have watched the parakeets for a long time. I know you are enjoying yourself. How much longer would you like to watch?" Pick a specific amount of time. One minute, two minutes. Time doesn't mean much to him at this age, but it does give him a sense of having control over when he stops this particular activity. A toddler likes to be in control. When someone like Mom arbitrarily stops him from doing something, more than likely it will make him angry.

An active child will find it difficult to sit still for any length of time. If you find your toddler is too active to be confined in someone's living room during a visit, for example, arrange to visit your friends at the park so that your child can run and climb. (You won't have to visit with your friends in the park forever.) Keep store trips to an absolute minimum. Stores are terrible places for youngsters, even under the best of circumstances. Children hate department stores because there are lots of interesting things for them to do—things to touch, escalators to ride up and down—but they aren't allowed to, and this makes them frustrated and angry.

You should not expect a toddler to have an interest in cleaning up after himself. Many parents feel that they are being run ragged just from the effort of coping with the chaos and mess that a toddler creates, and some unnecessary conflicts can erupt because of this. Try to convey to the child the idea that things have to be put back after they've been played with. This is merely planting the seeds for orderliness later in life; he won't really be capable of it now. Although you can engage the child in playful participation, it's important to assume the responsibility yourself for cleaning up. By the way, many children don't develop a sense of orderliness and neatness until after toilet training.

Whining

Recently, a mother called me in despair. "I'm nearly out of my mind," she said. "My two-year-old daughter whines all the time lately. It's such an awful sound. Every time she does it, I can just feel my own anger rising in me. How can I get her to stop whining?"

My theory about whining is that it is a form of anger, muffled or suppressed. The child may or may not be aware of feeling angry, but she is nevertheless acting on this anger by whining. She does this rather than having a tantrum or breaking things. It is often the "well-behaved" children who begin to whine. Somewhere along the line they have learned to suppress angry outbursts. Not surprisingly, many parents find whining worse to listen to than overt displays of anger. It's maddening because you really can't get a handle on the source.

The first thing to do is to help the child unlock the anger. If you don't, the anger will remain suppressed, but it won't really go away. Whining is a way of keeping a lid on it, and you have to help your child get that lid off. There are ways to eliminate the whining, but punishing a child for it will only keep that anger more suppressed. Rather, your goal should be to help her allow the anger to come to the surface.

Keep track of the circumstances that cause your child to whine; they may give you a clue as to what is frustrating her. If you can identify constant sources of frustration, you may be able to eliminate some of them. The whining may then go away, because you will have done away with the reason for the anger.

A child's constant whining may indicate a general feeling of dissatisfaction—an overall discontent with her life at the moment. Try to evaluate the nature of your relationship with her to see just what is making her feel so frustrated. I don't mean to suggest that your child is justified in feeling frustrated all the time. Some children whine habitually when they are tired, or simply because they can't always have what they want. But there may be some underlying cause that you will be able to ferret out by investigation, and may, after a time, help eliminate from the child's life.

Some people have suggested that parents should ignore a child's whine. I think it's impossible to ignore whining because it's so irritating. It also doesn't help the child much. You can aid the child, however, by labeling for her exactly what she's doing. Perhaps she is totally unaware of the fact that she's whining. Say to her, "The sound you are making now is called whining. I think you must be angry about something." By calling attention to the sound she is making, you will be helping her identify this behavior in the future. You are also calling attention to the underlying anger, and you may be able to help her identify its source. If you are fairly certain of the reason for the anger, you might add, "I think you are angry because you wanted to go to the store to buy ice cream and I said that we had to stop off at the cleaners first." Occasionally that awareness may help relieve the child's frustration and resultant anger.

I don't think such tactics will work every time, but by finding out the source of the child's anger, making her aware of the sound she makes when she whines, and helping her organize her thoughts about why she feels frustrated, you may be able to lessen episodes of whining. Of course, once you unlock the source of the child's frustration, you'll have to deal with her outward expressions of anger. But as one mother once said, "At least I can deal with the anger. It's something I can get my hands on."

Being a Pest When Mom or Dad Is on the Phone

When the phone rings, you can be certain that a child will do something obnoxious. I have heard hundreds of parents say that as soon as they get on the phone all heck breaks loose.

The telephone seems to be one of the greatest enemies for children. To have a parent physically present but mentally with someone else is experienced as an offense. If you are with the child, the child wants you 100 percent. A child's misbehavior is a way of saying, "If you're talking to someone else, you'd better darn well notice that I'm here. I want all of your attention." To make sure he gets your attention, he'll go into the bathroom and sprinkle bubble-bath crystals all over the floor.

You'll have an easier time of it if you remember to put your expectations in line with the child's capabilities and emotional needs. Be aware of the fact that you will not change your child's mind about needing you when you are on the phone. What will have to change is the length of time you spend on the phone, as well as how you handle your child while you are talking. This will also hold true for emergency calls, by the way. A toddler can't distinguish between a social call and an emergency call, and simply telling him that it's an emergency will do little good.

Armed with these ideas, here's what to do: When the phone rings, say to your child, "Oh, the phone is ringing. Come on, let's go answer it. Let Mommy say hello first." If it's someone the child can say hello to, tell the caller, "Hi, Aunt Julia. Billy would like to say hello." Meanwhile, Billy is right next to you, and he's not being excluded. Let the child talk and then tell him you're going to talk for a minute, after which he can say goodbye. This won't work every time, but even if it works 10 percent of the time, that's 10 percent fewer episodes of mischief you'll have to deal with.

Another approach I suggest is to bring the child over to the telephone with you when you answer it, all the while keeping your arm around him. This is partly to restrain him, but also to make physical contact. You're suggesting by this gesture that your attention is still with him, which is really the issue.

A third approach is also possible. If you anticipate that the phone might ring, have an activity nearby that you know will interest your child. Perhaps he can color at your feet or play with a set of building blocks. The key, of course, is to keep the conversation brief. Very rarely will a toddler allow you a long conversation without interrupting you or getting into trouble. There's no reason you can't say to the caller, much like anyone in an office situation might, "Excuse me, but can I call you back in a few minutes?"

The fourth approach to the problem is to make use of one of our modern conveniences: the answering machine. Many parents I know who have answering machines in their homes use them to avoid just this problem. If you are engaged in a game with your toddler and you know that interrupting it will cause a mini crisis, simply allow the machine to take the message and call the person back when your child is in bed or occupied with something that doesn't require your full attention.

Repetitive Behavior

Many children go through a phase at this age during which they like to repeat certain kinds of activities. Some children, for example, will eat only certain foods for months. Others will insist on wearing only purple clothes every day. There is a kind of comfort in a repetitive activity. It's a form of ritualistic behavior that gives the child a feeling of security. Occasionally children will constantly open or close doors or want to go up and down curbs or stairs. In such cases, there is also an element of mastery involved.

Take solace in the fact that the repetitive behavior won't last forever. Eventually your toddler will change. Until that time, try to demonstrate self-control. To stay calm, allow him to pursue the activity, but don't let it get to the point where it's driving you batty and you feel as if you're going to scream. Before that happens, do something dramatic to distract your child. Perhaps he's banging on a door. You could drop a pot loudly on the kitchen floor. In all likelihood, your son will come toddling in to find out what happened. "Look at that!" you can say, and get him interested in some other activity.

When you have to go visiting and you're concerned that your child's repetitive behavior will be an annoyance, bring along a toy that will distract and interest him while he is there. If it's a person you know well who won't mind the child opening and closing a door repeatedly or going up or down stairs, then let him. Try to stay calm, and remember, it won't last forever.

Bedtime Troubles

One of the most difficult issues to resolve with a toddler is bedtime. Your long-term goal is not to squash your child's independence and determination not to go to bed willingly or to fall asleep gracefully, but rather to help him toward the self-discipline of being able to put himself to sleep without distress.

One mother of a two-year-old told me recently that her son had begun screaming when put to bed. To get him to stop, she would lie down on the floor with him in his corner or bring him to bed with her. If she didn't, he would climb out of his crib and run around the house.

Lying down on the floor with a toddler or allowing him into your bed isn't a good way to get a child to conform to a bedtime ritual. Instead, place a comfortable chair in his room and sit there when it is time for him to go to sleep. That way, you will be in the room with him, so he can be comforted by your presence, but you can begin to distance yourself from him so that he will learn to fall asleep on his own, without getting overwrought.

By the way, it isn't necessary that the child sleep in his bed. If he'd prefer to sleep on a mattress on the floor, let him. If your child is comfortable there, why not? Many children develop idiosyncratic preferences for sleeping places.

When the bedtime ritual is over, tuck your child in and sit down in a chair for a while. Do something while you are in the chair. Perhaps you could write a letter or fold some laundry or read. Of course, this may be a bit more difficult if you want to keep the room darkened so that your child can sleep better, but the point is that you needn't sit there idle, just staring at your child. Even if you fall asleep, at least he will be lying down and you will be in the chair. If he climbs up, comfort him calmly and return him to his bed. Be persistent but calm! This first phase may take as long as a week or ten days before he finally accepts that you are not going to lie down with him. This is a crucial step because it establishes an initial separation, upon which you will be able to build.

An intermediate phase in this procedure is for you to move around in the room. From time to time get up and do something quiet, like straightening a drawer or rearranging some toys. Be sure to move in and out of his visual field. That way he becomes accustomed to your presence but is not totally dependent on seeing you. Again, it may take another week or more for him to adjust.

Once you have done this, you will have accomplished a great deal, and the next step will be much easier. The goal in the next phase is to be able to leave the room for short periods. In the beginning, say to your son, "I'll be back in a second. I just have to go to the bathroom," or "I just have to get another book." Leave the room, count to ten, and then walk back in. Sit down and say to him, "See, I came back." That's all. Do this for four or five nights. Gradually increase the time so that you are leaving for a minute or two. The increases should be barely noticeable to your son, but should ultimately lead to your long-term goal— being able to leave the room once and for all. Toward the end, you might begin saying, "I'll check in on you in a couple of minutes." Do not try to trick him. Be sure to come back repeatedly until he falls asleep. If all goes well, you can look forward to a time when you will be able to say "Goodnight," simply and lovingly.

Temper Tantrums

A child having a temper tantrum can be a scary sight. The screaming can be terrible. A child will pull his hair, hit himself, throw himself on the floor, and he might even bang his head. The temptation is to yell at the child to stop, but yelling or spanking him won't help at all.

The first thing to do is to take a look at all the incidents that stimulate a temper tantrum to see what they have in common. It's usually frustration. At a later age, when a child's speech is more developed, he will be able to verbalize much of this frustration. "I'm frustrated. This darn thing keeps falling down," he might say, or, "Hey, Mom, don't you hear me? I'm calling you." Being able to say clearly what's bothering him will make things much easier, and he won't have to throw his toys or scream. For the moment, however, his frustration is compounded by the fact that he can't adequately communicate what's bothering him so. What he's doing now is the most direct way of telling you that he's extremely annoyed. Keep in mind that one of the most typical reactions to frustration is aggression or anger. Your child gets angry; he can't verbalize his anger, so he throws a fit.

When a child is in the middle of a temper tantrum, there is little you can do but see him through it. It is virtually impossible to stop a tantrum once it has started. If the child is in a safe place—a well-carpeted room, for example—simply leave the room and let the child have his fit. A toddler has only so much energy to expend, and eventually the tantrum will die down.

If the child begins to hit himself or bang his head seriously on the floor, or if you are in a place that is not safe—a public building with marble floors, for example—you will then have to restrain him. To do this, envelop the child in your arms firmly but not punitively. Hold him with his back against your front. Put yourself on automatic and say, quite monotonously, "Take it easy. Calm down. I don't want you to hurt yourself." When the tantrum is over, refrain from any big hugging and kissing scenes. It is not necessary for you or the child to feel guilty about the tantrum. Simply acknowledge that it is over and tell the child you're glad he's feeling better.

Although it is not often possible to stop a tantrum once it has started, you can work to avoid at least some of them. You will not be 100 percent successful. Almost all children have tantrums during this age. But if you give the child another way to express his anger and frustration, you may be able to keep such tantrums to a minimum.

A child who is able to express his frustration verbally may not have to resort to a tantrum. You can help him do this by talking to him in full sentences. Avoid saying "no" when his behavior alarms, distresses or annoys you. Rather, give the child a complete explanation: "That is a dangerous object," or "This is sharp and can hurt you," or "That's very fragile, so we must be careful." By doing so, you teach the child to attend to the full explanation, and over time, such explanations will become part of his internal repertoire.

Anticipating that your child will have a tantrum if he is frustrated may also help limit the number and severity of such outbursts. To the extent that you can, try to reduce the child's frustration, and be aware that you are not always the source of it. Children often frustrate themselves, and there is very little you can do about that except possibly to see a situation coming and intervene. For example, if you have a hunch that your child is likely to become frustrated because his blocks keep falling over, you can offer to help by showing him another way of building the structure he had in mind. If he throws the blocks and gets angry, put the toys aside. Pick the child up and talk to him and try to comfort him. If that doesn't work, then just sit him down in a quiet spot and say, "Let's have a little quiet time here." If that doesn't work, let him scream it out, and leave it at that.

The important thing to remember here is that a tantrum is not an occasion for punishment. Although often quite distressing—who wants to watch a child behave in such an angry and aggressive manner?—it is really analogous to a whistling kettle letting off steam. The child has to be allowed to express his frustration in some manner. Until he has speech and is able to demonstrate a bit more self-control, temper tantrums must be expected.

Sibling Rivalry

Sibling rivalry is quite common during the toddler age if a new baby arrives on the scene. A somewhat distraught mother described this full-blown case:

> I have a two-and-a-half-year-old son and a nine-month-old daughter. My son, of course, has a lot of toys. But if the baby touches any toy, even a toy my son doesn't appear to be interested in, he has a

fit. It seems as if he's screaming and grabbing at her all the time. I came home from work the other night, and the baby-sitter had had to divide the den by putting a couch in between them. How can I get him to stop screaming at her and to stop grabbing everything away from her?

It's not at all unusual for the boy to behave this way. It may seem that he is overreacting every time his sister touches one of his toys. After all, he doesn't need all his toys every moment, so why should it bother him? He *is* overreacting, but why? And to what?

On the surface, he does mind that the toy is being touched. The toy is his. His sister, at nine months, is obviously able to get around and get into his possessions. She can now intrude upon his territory by touching and messing up his toys. On a deeper level, however, she has irrevocably intruded upon much more important territory—his once-exclusive relationship with his parents. His distress at having his toys invaded is symbolic of the much deeper distress caused by the invasion of this all-important relationship by a very demanding infant.

His behavior is common, and frankly I am more surprised by parents who tell me about older siblings who never had a problem with a new baby. In those cases, I often wonder if the distress won't come out in some other indirect and perhaps less desirable way.

Imagine, for a moment, the distress from the child's point of view. You're two years old and suddenly a baby comes into the house for good. Mom is very busy nursing or feeding the baby, and other people are making a big fuss over her. The baby takes up a lot of time and is very irritating. She cries, and people rush to comfort her. She wakes you up during the night. Mom is too tired to pay much attention to you, and she seems to expect you to be more independent than you used to be. On top of everything else, Mom and Dad seem to love this little baby just as much as they used to love you. No wonder, then, that you become overwrought when this new baby has the audacity to touch things that belong to you.

Now compound this distress with the intense sense of "me and mine" that I discussed at the beginning of this chapter. A toddler, as you will recall, has a very difficult time coping with the idea that something that is not in his immediate possession can still remain his. Therefore, a baby picking up his toy is a gesture that threatens his sense of possession. He feels that he's lost it, and that it's not his anymore. A two-and-a-half-year-old is just beginning to come to terms with the concept of owning something and perhaps "lending" it to someone else. Most children this age are not terribly good at it. If you add this to the feeling of being displaced by the new baby, you can see why sharing space or toys is going to lead to a lot of tension.

So now that you know all that, what do you do? First of all, I don't think it's such a bad idea to separate siblings, if that is feasible. After all, children in different stages of development have different needs and communicate differently. Occasionally you can bring them together, but don't go out of your way to facilitate that. They are going to be around each other anyway, simply because they live in the same house.

If you can, invite a little friend over for your older child to play with so that he will have his own comrades. Parents often make the mistake of insisting that the older sibling treat the younger sibling as a friend. I think you can occasionally ask the older child to treat the younger one in a nice manner, but you shouldn't force them together. The reality is that they may not be friends for some years. This is often a dismaying fact for parents to face, but it is true nevertheless. Of course, you should foster the notion of family and promote the idea that members of the family look out for one another, but you can't make siblings love to play with each other.

One day when it is quiet, invite your older child to go through his toys with you to decide which ones he might not want anymore and might be willing to let the baby play with. You might even suggest that he put a sticker on all the stuff that is his, and help him put the toys on a high shelf so that the younger child can't get to them. Allowing your older child to have some control over his toys this way is better than just arbitrarily suggesting that he share them.

Should conflicts arise, and they probably will, in spite of all your precautions, you should say to your older child, "I know it is very annoying to you when your sister takes your things, but I'd rather that you not grab the toy away from her. Tell me and I will get it for you. I'd rather you didn't grab because it hurts her feelings. I try not to hurt your feelings, and I would rather you didn't hurt her feelings." The reason he grabs the toys rather than complain to you is that he wants to do something nasty to the baby. He's angry that the baby is around all the time.

With any luck, your older child will one day want to play with one of the baby's toys, and your lessons about sharing and not hurting her feelings will be reinforced. Suggest to him that you and he ask her if it is all right to borrow one of her toys. Although their communications are apt to be quite primitive, both children will get some practice in negotiation, which will be valuable as they grow older.

Toilet Training

Toilet training *is* a discipline issue, but is *never* an occasion for punishment. Your primary goal should be to help your child achieve *self-discipline* in this vital area.

I would suggest a number of tactics to help your child learn to use the toilet properly when he feels the urge. The first is to try putting him on the toilet or potty chair for one minute, about six or seven times a day. Do this for just one minute, and show him what one minute is on the clock or on a timer. This way he will get used to giving in to you and sitting on the toilet. If he doesn't urinate or have a bowel movement, say, "Okay, perhaps next time you will." Don't have a big conversation about it.

When he tells you himself that he has to go, take him into the bathroom and sit him on the toilet. Follow the same procedure.

If the child hasn't urinated or had a movement in the toilet, but you suspect that he really does have the urge, you might also try this experiment: Send him out of the bathroom without any underwear. Sometimes children are a little puzzled when they have to have a bowel movement or urinate and don't have a diaper or underwear on. They don't want to mess up the floor. This alone might motivate your child to go back to the bathroom or request his underwear. When it happens, immediately place him on the potty seat or toilet. Many repetitions may be necessary.

If you do send the child out without underwear and he relieves himself on the floor, you should say to him, "Hey, look, that's not the place for you to do this. You are not supposed to have a bowel movement or urinate on the floor. Try to remember." Don't make a very big deal about it, but allow your child to see some disappointment and some annoyance. Have the child help you clean it up, and then take him into the bathroom. Tell him that from now on, you want him to use the toilet. Be serious and stern, but try not to overdo it.

If your child does have an "accident," real or deliberate, always change him in the bathroom in a standing position. Don't lay him down on the floor or on a changing table. Make him wait in the bathroom for a minute so that it's a little boring. Look at your watch and call out, "I'll be in there in a minute. You just wait there for me." Wait sixty seconds, and then return to him. Children don't like to wait, and quite possibly the annoyance of it will be another motivation to use the toilet, which is much quicker.

Some parents use attendance in a day-care group or nursery school as an incentive, but I would caution against this. You may be unpleasantly surprised to find that your son has decided that toilet training is too big a price to pay for going to nursery school. Then you'll be left with no school and no toilet training.

Another drawback to using school as a motivator is that some children learn to withhold their stools while in school and continue to soil at home. They simply avoid the issue by not using the bathroom in school, and in that way toilet training never becomes a school problem. Very often such children generalize this tendency and retain for several days. They develop problems with constipation, and that, in turn, creates more training problems.

Be careful not to start toilet training too soon. Two and a half is considered the average age; sometimes girls are a bit earlier. Use this as a rule of thumb.

Be consistent. Don't become overwrought. Above all, don't *punish* the child. Time and practice and a great deal of patience are called for at this time. (Toilet-training problems during the preschool stage require somewhat different strategies and are discussed in the next section.)

Spitting

Spitting is a hostile act. Children learn how to scream, how to swear and how to spit. If a child spits out of anger, it's like uttering a profanity. When a writer wants to convey anger in his speaker, he will often use the phrase, "He spat out his words." For a child, the feeling is similar. Spitting can convey frustration and the momentary inability to deal with it.

If a child spits just once or twice, it may be merely an experiment. Perhaps he just learned how, or perhaps he saw a friend do it. If that's the case, you might prudently ignore it, or you might invite him into the bathroom to fill up a cup with water and spit into the sink. Not only does this put the activity under your control, but also it has the added effect of taking the charge out of the spitting.

Sometimes children playing outside will have a contest of who can spit the farthest. Or they may spit with glee, knowing it is daring and naughty. Usually older children engage in playground or schoolyard spitting, but if your toddler is doing it, employ the same tactics to try to neutralize the situation. Although you can't stop the child from spitting, you can defuse the act by saying, not without a sense of humor, "Boy, oh, boy, you guys are really disgusting. I can't think of anything more revolting than spitting all over each other. What a silly thing to do!"

Profanity

A toddler gets angry and frustrated. He uses a word to express his anger. You happen not to like the word, so you punish him for using it. You will have to find another way to handle this, however, because a toddler needs some opportunity to vent his annoyance. You don't want to close that off.

When a child this age uses profanity, don't make a big deal about it. If you do, you give the child more power. After all, it's only a word—one that won't do much harm to anybody. In fact, if you think about it, a nasty word is a step up from hitting or biting someone. So look at it as a sign of growth and development.

When your child uses the forbidden word in front of you, you needn't mention that you don't like the word; he already knows that. Instead, say to him, "You know, we've heard that word so many times before, it's really boring and tiresome. It's not a very polite word, but if you really feel you have to say it, go into your room and say it as many times as you want." More than likely, this will stop the behavior, and when he gets to his room, he might feel kind of silly saying it all by himself.

The second thing you can do when he says the word is to ask him what it actually means. Sometimes this really surprises a child. He knows it's a word that gets a rise out of everybody, but it's very likely that he doesn't know what it means. Once you tell him what it means, it will probably shock him, and he may even stop using it.

The primary goal here is to make the child understand just where and when he can use the word. Obviously he can use it outside the house, in his room or with his friends, if he wants to. But he may not use it around you or around other adults. The idea is to let him know that profanity is a matter of social acceptability, and not that he is bad for having such thoughts. Even world leaders have been known to utter expletives at inopportune moments!

When You Have to Leave Them . . .

You're getting ready to go to work. Your toddler pleads with you not to go. He worries, he cries, he begs for a thousand kisses. Although such scenes may tug at your heartstrings and may leave you with a residue of guilt, what your child is doing is actually quite normal and understandable. He feels bad that you're leaving him. He worries about when you'll be leaving him again. He stays put, but you come and go. He has no control over these comings and goings; to him they are unpredictable. Even if you tell him you have to leave at 8:30 every morning, he doesn't really know you're leaving until you start to get dressed. All of his anxieties and pleadings and tears are merely his way of coping with a difficult situation. Think of it from his point of view. Isn't it much easier, even as an adult, to be the one who leaves rather than the one who is left behind?

Your child is really addressing himself quite sensibly to the problem at hand. First he pleads with you to see if you will change your mind. When it becomes clear that you won't or can't, he expresses what he wants and what he is feeling. He cries. Then he asks for kisses and hugs—he wants reassurance that you love him and that you won't forget about him while you are gone. A child believes that if you love a person, you stay with that person 100 percent of the time. So if you leave him, he becomes anxious.

Anxieties are not always bad for a child, but sometimes it's difficult to tell which ones will strengthen a child and which will cause problems. We can predict that some of the more traumatic anxieties might cause serious trouble, but this isn't one of those instances—particularly if you are sure that his crying stops once he is in another's care, and if you are confident that he is receiving good care in your absence. Frankly, such a situation is much more alarming if the child isn't wrestling with his feelings, or if you are ignoring them.

Don't be tempted to gloss over your leaving. And certainly don't lie to your child. Tell him the truth, give him the thousand kisses he asks for, and tell him you'll be thinking about him all day. I would even suggest that you bring some little treat or toy home for him. The toy is a visible symbol that you were indeed thinking of him during the day.

When They Have to Leave You . . .

Sometimes you stay put, but your child has to leave you to go to day care. She cries when she leaves you and she cries when she gets to the center. What do you do?

You might try to ease the transition by first talking to your child about the day-care center when the two of you are alone together. Get her to express some of her feelings about it. Find out, if you can, whether there is some specific source of worry: Is she afraid of the bathroom? Of having the wrong kind of lunch pail? Of someone teasing her?

Next, help her to make friends with some of the other children by inviting several of them over, one by one, so that they can play together. Do this as soon as possible. If she has a friend, she may become more comfortable at the center because she'll already have someone there with whom she can play or just sit next to.

And last, allow her to bring some things from home to the center to remind her of home and of the security there. Sometimes a photograph of you or your spouse can be comforting. A set of keys to keep in her pocket or even a small edible treat, if it is permitted, can be a source of reassurance.

THE PRESCHOOL YEARS:
BECOMING A DEPUTY

By the time a child is in the preschool stage—from three to five years old—her social skills, language and physical coordination are much more advanced than they were in the toddler stage. These three attributes help the child to be more socialized and to have somewhat more self-control than she did just a year earlier. As her parent, you will find that your child is better able to conform to routines, to understand rules and regulations that govern certain activities and to negotiate and communicate with you. Gradually, because of her greater social interaction with friends at play and in nursery school, the preschool-age child begins to learn that it might be more fun to go along with someone else's ideas for a change.

In tandem with this development, the child also begins to acquire the beginnings of empathy—a tremendous achievement and one that will, in the near future, make your interactions with her a lot less conflicted. Once a child is able to understand someone else's point of view—to see, as it were, from the other side of the table—she can then become more compliant, more thoughtful, more considerate and even more generous.

By being able to imagine how another child or a parent feels as a consequence of her actions, your child may begin to exhibit restraint or self-control ,in areas where she previously had very little or none. Self-control is a main ingredient of self-discipline.

The world of the preschooler and the world of the toddler are vastly different. The preschooler, as opposed to the toddler, is now more likely to want to do things with other children and adults. Although the preschooler will continue to see herself as the center of the universe and want things to go her way most of the time, she is not as obsessively self-centered as she was a few short months ago. As her parent, you can begin to introduce more rational explanations with the real hope that your child will absorb them. By now, for example, the child has had enough experience to realize that things do break, and that if something is broken she won't have it anymore. You can now ask a child to be very careful with an item because it is delicate, and have a fairly reasonable expectation that the child will try, to the best of her ability, to treat it with care because she *understands* the consequences. Previously, such an explanation was likely to be of little use as a deterrent.

You will also observe during this period that your preschooler enjoys taking on adult roles—probably yours, in fact. If you shave, your son is likely to want to pretend shaving in the mirror. If you wear nail polish, your daughter may begin to bug you about putting some on her nails. If you're vacuuming the rug, or changing the oil in the car, or folding the laundry or paying bills, your preschooler is likely to want to become part of the activity, mimicking what you do. Of course, it is easier to get a job done if you can do it by yourself, but resist that temptation during this age, and try, as one insightful parent called it, to "deputize" your child. By allowing her to engage in appropriate "adult" activities, you give her a chance to practice her skills and encourage her to be independent, yet you still can oversee the activity and keep her out of trouble by remaining in control of the situation. If she wants to polish the silverware or vacuum the rug or help you wash the car, permit her to work with the real objects and to perform the real activities. Your task may take you a bit longer than you'd like, but in the process you will be guiding and educating your child and giving her valuable experience.

The flip side of this charming and exciting taking on of adult roles, however, is that you will discover that your child, in her eagerness to be so like you, becomes competitive with you. In fact, part of her behavior may stem from a desire to supplant you altogether. During this stage of development, parents often find themselves embroiled in bitter disputes with their preschoolers, who always want to be the boss, to win every argument, to dictate the rules, to come out on top of every physical tussle or race or competition, and generally to tell their parents what to do. "I told you a million times," your preschooler will sigh in an exaggerated, exasperated tone, "not *those* socks." Or your child, engaged in a game of checkers with you in which it becomes momentarily apparent that she might not win, suddenly changes the rules. Or, upon losing the game, falls over backward on the floor, sobbing hysterically because you didn't play "fair." At times you may even see an overdeveloped sense of injury—in the midst of a gentle wrestling match, your preschooler may suddenly pull away and shrick, "You're trying to hurt me!"

The preschooler's fiercely competitive streak can lead to a great deal of tension in the household if the parents do not defuse it. During this period, parents often make the mistake of thinking that it's more important that the child learn the rules of a game and that she learn to play fairly, regardless of her own heartbreak at losing. My feeling about this tender stage of development, however, is that it's more important to help support the child's notion that she is strong, competent and capable. As best you can, go along with her rules and try not to be overly concerned about her bossiness at this age. Rather than feel threatened by the child's desire to be in charge and by what may well be obnoxious pushiness, see it as an important phase of her development. In so doing, you may be better able to tolerate it.

As your child begins to imitate you and your adult role—often trying to go you one better—you will also observe that she will begin to imitate your speech and vocabulary. The preschooler who says with a sigh, "I told you a million times . . ." is probably parroting her parent, but so is the child who chirps up, *"I've* got a good idea . . ." Although you will find that many of the reprimands you have given your child are thrust rather rudely back at you, you will also find that your child has more interest in verbal negotiation than ever before. You will get more arguments from your preschooler, but encapsulated within these arguments will be the beginnings of an understanding of what compromise and negotiation are all about. The preschooler who suddenly says, "I've got a good idea" or "I've got a good deal," meaning that she is ready to negotiate according to her rules, is practicing for the future, when she will be expected to negotiate and compromise often with you and with her peers.

To the extent that you are able, try to foster these early attempts at deal making and negotiation, even if you have to give in more than you might want to. The deals, you can be sure, will be heavily weighted in favor of your preschooler, but giving her an opportunity to see how negotiation works and to feel that she is an effective and competent deal maker will promote, rather than inhibit, negotiating in the future. It can get a bit out of hand, and on many occasions you may feel like sending her to sleep-away law school even before she's completed kindergarten!

At this age you may also notice that your child has a pronounced interest in sex. Questions about birth and reproduction are common. Masturbation is frequent. Playing doctor may become a favorite game. These matters can be upsetting to parents. You may find yourself feeling angry and flustered. Some adults would prefer to think that sexual interest does not begin until puberty. But this is not so. In fact, some psychologists refer to the preschool years as a "first adolescence."

Parents sometimes worry that their child's sexual curiosity in the preschool phase will lead to promiscuity in a few short years unless something is done about it now. If you think sexuality is bad, you may be inclined to instill guilt. If you believe sexual curiosity is the beginning of a downward spiral toward hedonism, you may become unnecessarily strict. When parents are embarrassed, they often react in an effort to lower their own anxiety. My guess is that much of the trouble we have as parents in dealing with childhood sexuality stems from a tendency to superimpose adult motives and prohibitions on our children. We also tend to repeat the manner in which our own parents handled these issues. In a way, this brings us to the heart of the developmental matter of the preschool years.

We are all familiar with the notion that we repeat our parents' actions when we ourselves become parents. This tendency is part of a process of identification that begins in the preschool years, when children engage in a good deal of mimicry and role-playing. In so doing, they are incorporating our traits, gestures, attitudes and beliefs. Imitation leads the way to internalizing our rules and regulations—our prohibitions and values. Identification means our children become like us.

The process of identification is not complete for many years. In fact, some identification goes on throughout our lives. At various points it is heightened—most notably during adolescence, when hero worship of movie and music idols, sports stars and political figures takes over in a large way—not unlike the "superhero" craze we see in preschoolers. At times of stress, especially when loss is involved, a disproportionate degree of identification may occur: Sometimes, in trying to hold on to the person we have lost, we attempt to become that person.

During preschool identification, a child begins to develop an inner sense of right and wrong and the stirrings of moral judgment. But this primordial conscience is not very reliable yet. It does not yet equip the child to overcome temptation consistently or comprehend mutuality, that is, concern for others, or reciprocity.

The means by which you control your child plays a major role in the kind of self-control she will eventually have. If you are a harsh and punitive parent, your child is likely to have a tough time developing an inner set of controls that she can live with comfortably. An understanding and supportive approach to discipline at this phase instead enables your child to develop a moderate, more balanced set of inner standards. The rudimentary conscience your child begins to form at this stage is an important step toward socialization and greater self-discipline.

REALISTIC EXPECTATIONS, PARENTAL GOALS AND TECHNIQUES FOR PRESCHOOLERS

REALISTIC EXPECTATIONS

1. The child has somewhat more control than in the toddler stage.
2. The child is better able to conform to rules.
3. The child begins to develop empathy.
4. The child has better ability to negotiate.
5. The child is more social and less self-centered.
6. The child can better attend to rational explanations.
7. The child has a better understanding of the concept of consequences to actions.
8. The child will try on adult roles.
9. The child may compete with the parent of the same sex.
10. The child may be bossy with peers or parents.
11. The child has a pronounced interest in sex.
12. The child has a beginning (though not yet reliable) sense of right and wrong.

PARENTAL GOALS

1. Support your child's notion that she is strong, competent and capable.
2. Help your child learn to conform when appropriate.

TECHNIQUES

1. Deputize your child when possible.
2. Foster early attempts at negotiating and deal making.
3. Offer the child rational explanations.
4. Allow the child to express her feelings.
5. Turn undesirable actions into desirable ones.
6. Ease competition between you and your child.
7. Give a child opportunities to satisfy her curiosity.
8. Build in extra minutes for daydreaming and distraction when trying to get your child to accomplish a task.
9. Help your child label his feelings.
10. Employ distraction.
11. If possible, offer alternatives rather than reprimands.
12. Offer your child advance notice.

COMMON PROBLEMS IN THE PRESCHOOL YEARS

The Strong-Willed Child

Life is often a series of struggles when you have a preschooler. Children become very rigid at times and unswerving in what they want, even if what they want is not realistic or acceptable. Because they are sometimes so strong-willed, it is impossible to avoid battles and arguments, regardless of how calm you are and how much you try to offer them explanations. You can do everything right, and yet still have a fight on your hands.

There aren't always easy answers to the conflicts that erupt between preschoolers and their parents. Take the case of a four-year-old girl who falls in love with a certain item of clothing—say, a dress—and doesn't want to take it off, *ever*. She screams if you try to wash it. She wants to sleep in it. Even though your explanations are quite rational—you do have to wash it sometimes—she doesn't want to relinquish it. What else can you do? Let her wear the filthy dress? You can perhaps do that for a time, but eventually she will have to take the dress off and the inevitable will happen. No matter what you do, she is almost destined to get upset and cry and carry on. You can't really avoid these kinds of struggles.

However, it doesn't mean that you can't *try* to avoid them; you can employ a variety of techniques, such as offering rational explanations for your behavior, allowing the child to experience the power of having her own decisions listened to and respected (up to a point), having tremendous patience when the child refuses to cooperate and beginning to allow her to live with the consequences of her actions and decisions.

Preschoolers find it very difficult to make decisions and stick with them. The reason for this is that they want everything. They want the power of making choices, but then don't like the choices they've made because they want *all* the options. Preschoolers are greedy that way. They overreach in many respects. As an adult, you know that if you make a left turn, you can't make a right, but a four-year-old doesn't like the idea of having to give up the option of the right turn just because she chose the left. In a sense, what she wants to do is go back and make the right turn, too. That she cannot is a hard lesson to learn, and your child is not going to learn it immediately. More than likely, it will take her a while to settle down—and in the meantime you're going to have some struggles.

I suggest that you begin to allow your child to experience the consequences of some of her choices. For instance, suppose your daughter wants to wear a dress even though it is too cold outside. Fine. You explain to her that it's cold, it's wintertime, and that during this season, it's more sensible to wear pants because there's a danger her legs will get chilly. Perhaps the nursery school has suggested to parents that children wear sweaters and warm clothes in winter. All to the good. This allows you to read the rules and regulations from a piece of paper. Explain to your child the consequences of her actions, then step aside. You have given her a rational explanation, you have set forth whatever external criteria exist, and now you can let her make her own choice. Unless you fear she will get frostbitten or will catch cold, allow her to wear the dress if she insists.

As a parent you have to protect your child from harm, but if harm is not involved, help the child learn to make good judgments by allowing her to practice this way.

Take the example of the child who wants Daddy to tuck her in, then changes her mind and wants Mommy to do it instead. You might be able to solve the problem by sharing the job—although if she is in a mood to demonstrate her newfound decision-making powers, this may not satisfy her. You can go along with perhaps one change of mind, but don't indulge her "revolving door" notion of who should tuck her in. Again, allow your child to live with the consequences. If she requests her father, her father should go in. If she changes her mind, he might simply say, and not without some humor, "Oh, no, you asked for me, and here I am. I'm afraid since you asked for me, and I came, that I'm the one to do it. Tomorrow night you can have a chance to ask for Mom."

At times you will come across a child who doesn't want to conform to anything—a real rugged individualist. In such a case, your task as a parent is to help the child toward conformity and try simultaneously to reduce the frustration both you and he are feeling.

Some nonconformist or defiant behavior may suggest that a child is reacting to frustration. In a very confining or restrictive environment, an active child may become very reactive—that is, he may test you time and time again because he is annoyed that you inhibit him from fully experiencing his urges. Such a child must have some opportunity to satisfy his active curiosity—with your kind cooperation and supervision.

Quite possibly the activities the child wants to experience are not so terrible in and of themselves. Let's say your three-year-old son wants to turn the television on. He's not thinking about the fact that he might not do it gently or that he might break it. He is also interested in the toaster. What makes it tick? he wonders. Thoughts that playing with the toaster might be dangerous or that he might destroy it with his explorations don't really enter his mind. He may also want to climb on top of the refrigerator just to see what's happening up there—not realizing, of course, that he could fall and hurt himself.

The trick is to turn these undesirable activities into desirable ones. Accomplishing this will require that you provide supervision while giving your child more opportunities in and around the house to explore some of his interests. For example, if you find your preschooler tearing leaves off plants, you should explain to him that this is not acceptable and that it hurts and may destroy the plants. Then invite him to participate in some other activity that mimics it. Tearing the husks off corn, for instance, can be very satisfying to a child, or tearing pieces of paper into little shreds and then pasting them together to make a collage. Perhaps your child would like to make a big mess with water; take him into the bathroom, fill up the sink and supervise while he plays with bubbles, soap and plastic dishes.

If your child wants to climb up on top of the refrigerator, you will have to take him down, but you might say to him, "What were you looking for up there? Perhaps I can get it for you. If you just feel like climbing, let's find something safer to climb on." Or if he wants to turn the television on, you could stand by and teach him which buttons to push to get the channel he wants. He may still handle the TV roughly, but you will be there to help him. (Some children are more considerate and careful than others about such things. I know of many preschoolers who can quite competently manipulate the VCR!)

Remember, these measures will not work overnight. Given the intensely active natures of some children, you will have to expect some breakage. But these techniques may help 10 or 20 percent of the time, and will encourage both you and your child to move in the right direction. Even if you are not always successful in channeling your preschooler's explorations into more appropriate avenues, this method of discipline is far better than being overly punitive every time he does something you consider to be wrong. At three years of age, a child really lacks the kind of judgment that would stop him from tearing leaves off a plant or climbing on top of a refrigerator. Instead, help him to help himself by gently showing him how to conform and how to satisfy his curiosity safely. Instruction and careful guidance can make quite a bit of difference in your relationship. Don't assume that your child is intentionally destructive. Rather, see his behavior as a manifestation of ambition and curiosity that need direction and refinement.

Aggressive Behavior

Parents are often alarmed by bouts of aggressive behavior in their children. Aggressive behavior, however, is not unusual for a preschooler.

When your child does something aggressive, like throwing blocks at another child, tell him that what he is doing is hurtful. This will help him understand how other people feel when he is aggressive. Begin to talk about empathic responses. Even though he is still too young to appreciate this discussion fully, you call attention to your feelings as well as to his own feelings of hostility or anger. You may have to tell him to leave and go to his own room. If you comfort the child who has been victimized, your child may get the message that his undesirable behavior results in the loss of your attention. It will certainly not engender fonder feelings toward the victim!

These methods will not completely stop the aggression, but gradually, as he learns more self-control, your child will be able to keep himself in line.

One of the reasons a child acts in an aggressive manner may have something to do with his status and his desire for dominance. A small child who has few opportunities to dominate a situation often finds inappropriate outlets for this desire. The key to dealing with his aggression, therefore, is to find other ways for him to experience status and self-importance. Instead of hitting and pushing, he may find satisfaction in being given responsibility and a sense of being in charge. You can do this both by deputizing him to do certain adultlike things and by suggesting to him that you see his status as being very high.

Next, help your preschooler label his feelings. To do that, you'll have to be more direct than just suggesting that he may be angry or upset. Try to put things in focus: "Apparently you want to hurt Billy. You must not like Billy for some reason. I don't want you to hurt him." Obviously, you will have to remove your child from a situation like this one as well. Helping a child label his feelings is not an attempt to brainwash him. You can't convince a child that he should like another child or a younger sibling. You can and should, however, help him organize his feelings by inviting him to reveal them. Don't be tempted to put a judgment on those feelings. He's entitled to them, as unappealing to you as they might be. Simply say, "You obviously don't like Billy. You don't have to play with him. But you may not hurt him either. If you don't want to be nice, then don't. Just ignore him. We'll do something else. Sit by my side here and you can color or play with your truck."

Undoubtedly there will be times when you will have to reprimand your child for being aggressive or hostile. But you'll also need to have a little understanding about his reaction. No one likes to be reprimanded. When you reprimand your child it makes him angry, and he shows that anger. You shouldn't shut off this expression. If you were to succeed, where would his anger go? Permit him to get some of the rage off his chest. If he shouts or makes a fist and a couple of threatening gestures, view it not as insubordination, but as a rather innocuous and controlled release. Simply say, "I know you are angry. It's understandable that you are angry because you don't like my having to reprimand you."

Asking an angry child nicely to calm down implies criticism of his behavior; he may find such criticism hard to take. I think you'll find that you'll have an easier time if you employ distraction rather than direct commands or criticisms. It is sometimes useful to point out to a child that there are other ways to do particular things. Offer him alternatives instead of reprimands. (This won't always work, since he would probably prefer to think his way is best. Don't we all?)

Children who demonstrate exuberant or aggressive behavior often settle down once they begin attending nursery school because it is more organized than home, with its hierarchy, authority figures and more regimented schedule. Children often benefit from the discipline of belonging to such a group and of having to conform to the rules.

Dawdling, Procrastinating and Dillydallying

I often get calls from distressed parents asking me how to speed up their preschoolers so that everyone can get to school or work on time. Part of the problem, I tell parents, is that preschoolers are easily distracted by small things that interest them, so it's hard for them to stay directed toward a goal. Even though your child may have every intention in the world of cooperating with you, something else will catch her eye. Perhaps she'll decide as she is brushing her teeth that it would be more fun to fill up the sink and put some soap in. Before you know it, five minutes have gone by and she has experimented with the soap, but she hasn't brushed her teeth. Or you'll ask her to put her shoes on and she'll begin to do so, but the cat will meander by, and she will decide to tickle it.

Built into the problem is a child's concept of time and logic. Children experience time subjectively, much as adults sometimes do (the extremely boring lecture that seems to go on for hours; the especially stimulating conversation that shoots by in a flash). When you ask a preschooler to get dressed, more than likely the child thinks she can play with her toys or daydream and yet still have time to get ready and be in the car when she's supposed to be. The concept that certain tasks take a certain amount of time to accomplish is meaningless to her.

The problem is exacerbated when preschoolers discover that they can now dress themselves. Yet though the spirit is willing, they lack the necessary skill to do it as quickly as we often wish they would. Nevertheless, dressing oneself is an important step toward independence and self-reliance and should be fostered, not interfered with.

To do this and still make it to work promptly, I suggest that you leave more than ample time for the task—with extra minutes built in for daydreaming, distraction and getting the shirt on backwards or the shoes on the wrong feet. To ease your child's task and your own frustration, lay out the clothes the night before, allowing your child some choices. "Do you want to wear the red shirt tomorrow or the blue shirt?" you might ask. Never open the closet and say, "What do you want to wear tomorrow?" Such a vast choice is too difficult for a preschooler, in addition to which you may find her making a hopelessly inappropriate choice.

Select clothing with easy on-and-off features. Zippers and buttons may prove to be too difficult for novice dressers. Also make sure that shirts can be easily pulled over the head without assistance. You can also help your preschooler by pointing out that labels generally go in the back and by setting out her shoes pointing away from her with the left and the right in the correct places.

It's a good idea to remind a child at five-minute intervals about the task at hand. Try to do this without nagging. Just check in on the child every so often and make sure she is progressing, even if at a slow pace. I would look kindly on procrastinating at this age, because preschoolers can't really help themselves to be faster than they are. Not all dawdling is bad. Dawdling can provide a time for creativity, for calm thinking, for reflection and daydreaming, all of which are important to the pre-schooler's development.

The child who won't walk along the street and who either balks and lingers behind or insists on being carried between her parents is engaging in another form of dawdling that can sometimes drive parents crazy. From the child's point of view, there's a great joy in feeling the support and power in her parents' arms. The thrill of having her full weight carried along seemingly effortlessly is very exciting. You may therefore indulge your child for a while, but when you finally have to put her down, be prepared to deal with the consequences of frustrating her. The same holds true for a request for one more story at bedtime or one more piece of candy.

If your child is one who insists on lingering behind, you might find that strolling ahead (if you're in a safe location) is effective on occasion. But ask yourself if you are willing to keep walking if your little one decides to sit down and smell the roses or play with an ant she's found. And keep in mind that you run the risk of conveying to her that you are willing to leave her behind, which can be very upsetting to a small child.

In the final analysis, you can use distraction or you can point to a goal; you might have to tolerate a tantrum, or you may simply have to pick your child up and carry her to where you are going.

Giving Up a Bottle

By the age of three, most children have given up the bottle. The most difficult ones to eliminate are those at nap and sleep time. If this has not been accomplished in toddlerhood, it should be at this stage.

Helping a child to give up a bottle is a matter of discipline, because the issue here is self-control. Your goal is to get your child to be able to fall asleep without the crutch of a nipple in her mouth or a bottle in her hands. You will have to do this gradually and with compassion and understanding. Think for a minute of your own habits and how difficult it would be to give them up. For a three-year-old, a bottle is a habit, and it will be as difficult for her to relinquish it as it would be for any adult to give up smoking or overeating.

The first thing to do is not to let your child fall asleep with the bottle in her mouth—at any age. New evidence tells us that such a habit can destroy baby teeth and can even damage future second teeth. Although you needn't be concerned about your child having a bottle per se, you should be concerned if she is falling asleep with it.

Eliminating the bottle at nap time will be relatively easy compared with eliminating it at night. At nap time, refrain from offering her a bottle. Right there she will be forgoing seven bottles a week. If you find that she doesn't take the nap without the bottle, eliminate the nap, too. At this age, most children begin to give up their naps anyway. If you find that she is very tired and falls asleep even without the bottle, all to the good. This suggests that she might also be able to fall asleep at night without the bottle.

As for the nighttime ritual, don't be concerned if your child doesn't give up the bottle altogether, but immediately change the routine so that she has to get up and brush her teeth after having it. In other words, let her have the bottle in bed, but then tell her she has to brush her teeth (explain why) and perhaps use the toilet as well. Then she can go to sleep. That is easier said than done. Remember, she has always known the bottle as company at bedtime. Removing it will upset her normal self-comforting routine. Expect a rough transition period. It will probably take her longer to fall asleep; she may grump and call to you many times. Try to be patient. Tell her you know it will be difficult for her at first, but that she will get used to it soon. By doing this you will be accomplishing two things: First, you will be eliminating the bad habit of falling asleep with milk in her mouth, which can destroy teeth; and second, you will be paving the way for her to fall asleep without holding that crutch.

If she wants to take the bottle outside the home, inform her in advance of your plan to curtail that habit. Then, on the prescribed day of an outing, remind her that the bottle can be used only at home at bedtime. By restricting its use to the house and to a fixed time, you will diminish her reliance on it. *No cold turkey, please!* Be very patient and proceed gradually. No one can tolerate the sudden removal of a security source.

At first that's all you should do. When your child starts nursery school, you will probably find that she will give the bottle up of her own accord once she discovers that few of the other children still rely on it.

When a Child Won't Eat

Mealtimes can become fraught with tension when parents become overly concerned about what a child of three or four is eating. Usually parents fear the child isn't eating enough, and they resort to everything from threats to cajolery to reverse the situation.

If your child isn't in any danger of malnutrition, don't get too upset about what she eats and how much. As long as she has already managed to live for three or four years without ill effects and your pediatrician remains unconcerned, you should stop putting pressure on her.

Eating is a very complicated issue. When you are an infant, your first experiences involve food—being fed every couple of hours. Those early encounters with food are social and emotional ones. They help you to develop a sense of who you are and how you feel about yourself.

They also affect your relationship to food as you grow older. Some adults confuse food with love, use food as a substitute when they are bored, eat when they are anxious or don't eat when they are depressed. Since a child's relationship to food can so easily become distorted, my advice is to make eating as pleasant an experience as possible and to reduce any tension she may be feeling about food.

Most important, don't get involved in feeding a child of this age. A four-year-old can feed herself if she is hungry and should be encouraged to be independent in this regard. Feeding a child who ought to be able to feed herself is very intrusive. If your child seems reluctant to eat what the family is eating at the dinner table, it might be wise to make a list of all the foods she does eat. Will she eat cereal? raisins? yogurt? bananas? bread? It's hard to imagine that there aren't any foods that will catch her fancy and stimulate her appetite—after all, she has been eating something all these years. Once you have formulated your list of foods she likes, make an effort to provide them—regardless of how inappropriate you think they are for a dinner. It really doesn't matter if she eats cereal for supper or hamburgers for breakfast. Your goal is to get her to enjoy eating and to relieve any tension attached to the issue of food. (Obviously this is easier to implement if you have only one child or only one picky eater. I'm not suggesting that you prepare seven different meals, merely that you ease up on rigid expectations.)

Some children perk up to food when they are allowed to prepare and cook it themselves. Getting involved in meal preparation gives them an extra investment in eating it. It's often comical to watch how avidly a youngster will eat food he has cooked himself—all the time praising it to the hilt. I once saw this happen with a four-year-old girl who hated vegetables. One day in nursery school, she made vegetable soup with her class. She not only loved the soup, but came home and insisted, to her mother's delight, that the two of them make it the next night for supper.

I'm reliably informed that the same principle holds true for vegetable gardens. If you're lucky enough to have a small plot of land on which to raise some vegetables, involve your child in the planting, tending and harvesting. Not only is it educational, but also it often gets a child to eat vegetables he wouldn't dream of touching if he didn't have this added investment in them.

Finally, I suggest that you visit your local bookstore or library, where you will find a number of books on the subject of children and eating, many with helpful suggestions about how to prepare food more to a child's liking. Remember, your long-term goal is for your preschooler to become self-reliant. She must learn to make decisions about eating. Educating her about nutrition will help, but she also needs an opportunity to govern herself to some extent. This is when self-discipline comes into play. I urge parents not to use food as either a reward or a punishment. And please don't bribe a child to eat with the promise of desserts. Unless dessert is a healthy food like fruit or cheese that you'd be just as happy to see her eat with or without the meal, I'd advise forgoing it until the problem is resolved. Your child will become better able to regulate herself and employ self-control if eating behavior is kept free of strife and emotional stresses and entanglements.

Delayed Toilet Training

Not all children become toilet trained on cue. For some the issue lingers well into the preschool stage, and tension is likely to increase as parents gradually lose their patience—thus making the problem even more difficult to solve.

Parents are very likely to become angry for several reasons. On the surface, it's the mess and annoyance. Who wants to have to clean up two or three bowel movements a day, especially when your child is three and a half and you feel that such messes are unnecessary at this age? What nature helps us tolerate in an infant we find pretty irritating in a three-year-old. But parents become frustrated and worried for deeper reasons, too. In a parent's mind a child's inability to train himself represents a shortcoming, and nobody wants to think of his child as having a shortcoming. His playmates, after all, are probably trained. So what is wrong with your son? you worry. In addition to that, your fury rises to the surface because you can't control the situation, causing frustration and stimulating your anger.

Knowing the source of your anger may help you to deal with it. Expressing anger at this point in your child's toilet training is counterproductive, however. Before you can help your child to control his bowel movements, you have to get yourself under control.

Your child may offer some important clues to help you handle the issue. Perhaps he fears that he is going to fall into the toilet bowl, or doesn't want to flush his bowel movements away. Both of these worries are very common, and they don't necessarily mean that there is something terribly wrong with your child.

The fear of falling into the toilet bowl is an issue I think you have to see symbolically. Your child may actually think he can slip through the seat and into the bowl, but it is possible that this represents another, deeper fear—that somebody is going to get rid of him. This, you may say, is ridiculous: You never gave him that idea. But children this age have many irrational fears. To help your child with this one, say to him, out of the blue and not at a moment when you are both involved in toilet training, that sometimes kids think that their mommies and daddies are going to get rid of them, but you just want to make sure that he knows that you will never get rid of him, no matter what. That's all. Just a little reassuring statement that may help him voice something that's going on in his mind.

The basis for a fear of this kind is often the child's own inner wishes to get rid of you when he's angry. When a preschooler gets angry he may think to himself, "I'd like to flush you down the toilet." Consequently, he may fear that the same fate will befall him if he angers you. In a way, soiling himself is an expression of resistance to your efforts to get him to conform. His soiling may, therefore, be a sign of anger at your attempts to get him to do something he doesn't want to do yet.

Some children don't like to flush away bowel movements because they fear that a piece of them will be lost. The best way to handle this issue is to take your son to the library and find a children's book on the human body and the digestive process. Show your child the diagrams and explain that when we eat food, only part of it can be used by the body, and that the rest of it has to come out. There is no reason to keep the leftover part, and it's healthy to get rid of it. Tell him you understand that he might not want to flush it away, and that if he wants, you will leave it in the bowl for a while.

You might also point out that bowel movements have an odor that other people do not like. Remind your child that others may not want to be around someone who, at his age, doesn't use the toilet. I would not convey this idea to a younger child, because it can lead to feelings of shame about bodily functions. By three and a half, however, mild social pressure may be helpful.

Once you have dealt with these psychological issues, I think you will find that the practical matters of toilet training go much more smoothly. Bring the child into the bathroom every two hours to sit for two minutes at a time—give him a timer and show him the passage of the two minutes—and reward him verbally when he has a bowel movement by saying how pleased you are that he did it in the toilet (but don't go overboard with praise). Do not expect immediate results from your conversations. These thoughts take a while to work their way into a child's consciousness.

If toilet training is not accomplished by the age of four and soiling persists, you might consider a consultation with a child psychologist. A psychological evaluation may reveal problems that can be best handled by some play therapy or counseling. This would be preferable to endless power struggles and punishments.

Sibling Rivalry

Although sibling rivalry can occur at the toddler stage, it is also quite common during the preschool stage. Once the first child is toilet trained and in nursery school, parents often think about having another. Hence, the arrival of the sibling.

If you are having difficulties in this area, first of all, I suggest that you commiserate with your older child. Empathize with her about the inconvenience of having a tiny baby around. When you are alone with her, say that you know it can be tough sometimes for a three-year-old to have a tiny baby to cope with. Remark on how annoying it can be that the baby cries all the time and can't walk up the stairs by himself and needs to be carried. You may even go so far as to say to your child, "Oh, how dreary! The baby needs to be changed again. Isn't it irritating that he needs to be changed just as we were sitting down to read a book!" Although expressing irritation at a helpless baby may strike you as disloyal, keep in mind that the baby can't understand what you are saying, and that this speech is for your older child's benefit. Your goal is to make her a co-conspirator or assistant. Turn her into a sidekick by allowing her to help you with the baby. Three-year-olds can fetch blankets, help you change the baby and even hold the baby with your supervision. (Never leave three-year-olds alone with a baby. Not only do they lack necessary good judgment, but even the most seemingly loving and well-meaning siblings may suddenly act upon deep-seated hostilities they may have toward the baby.)

Second, when you and your older child are together alone I suggest that you read to her from some of the many good books available about new babies arriving in the home. Hearing storybook children express their fears and concerns at having a new baby in the house may help your child to organize and even to express some of her own thoughts about the matter.

Often older siblings will become especially defiant or will whine or scream a lot. This is a way of saying that no one is paying attention to them. When people scream, they're trying to get noticed. I wouldn't give an older child more attention while she is screaming, but later when you are alone together and things are quiet, say to her, in a nice way, "Sometimes I bet you feel like nobody is listening to you." Such a pronouncement, out of the blue like that, may encourage her to talk about what she is feeling. At the very least it will help relieve some of her frustration and may reduce her need to scream.

And finally, keep in mind that such a major adjustment in one's life takes time. It may be months or years before a child can accept a new baby. For the moment, avoid punishing her for her unpleasant behavior, and instead concentrate on empathizing with her and engaging her in conversations about her concerns and fears. When your child realizes that she is not going to be supplanted by the baby, she'll do much better. But she also must resign herself to the knowledge that the baby is here to stay and that you are all going to make room for the newcomer. That realization and acceptance requires a good deal of time and patient handling. Be aware, too, that some siblings have such vastly different temperaments that they may never become fast friends. In such situations, respect, tolerance and civility may be all you can expect. As children mature, they may lose some of the rivalry and learn to appreciate each other. This is, of course, an ideal that is not always realized.

Three's a Crowd

Typically during the preschool years, a child becomes jealous, possessive and uncomfortable when his parents are together, showing affection or just talking at the dinner table. One mother described her situation as follows:

> My three-year-old son is basically okay when he is with either me or my husband. When he has the undivided attention of either of us, he's no problem. But when my husband and I are together at dinner, my son becomes a terror. He starts hitting, pinching, kicking and grabbing the food off our plates. I usually feed my son earlier, and then my husband and I eat later in the evening. Sometimes if we are just sitting and talking at the table, he will come over to one of us—usually my husband—and start hitting him. We realize that it's hard for him to make the transition to being with us together, but what ends up happening more often than not is that we get no results and we end up yelling at him. And then he starts crying and making a big scene.

After being apart from each other all day, you and your spouse come together to reestablish your relationship. Your preschooler has safely had you all day, and now *Dad* comes home. Worse, you want to *talk* to Dad. Your child may feel that when the two of you have each other, he is left out. You're both sitting at the table, eating and talking, but he may feel that his status is minimized. So he interrupts. He nags you, and after a while, if you don't drop everything and pay attention to him, he'll assert himself in a more dramatic way—possibly by screaming, hitting or pinching.

The first thing to do is to talk with your child when the two of you are alone during the day. Say to him, "You know, when Daddy comes home I think you feel that he is interfering." Your preschooler may be relieved to hear you say that, because he may be feeling guilty about his jealousy and doesn't want to express it to himself. Then you can say, "When Daddy comes home, we can both talk to him. Remember that I'm Mommy and he's Daddy and that you're our son." He may not like your clarification of the relationships (after all, he may wish at times that Daddy did not exist at all), but bringing this out into the open will help him organize his own thoughts and accept the reality of the situation.

Second, give your child part of his dinner earlier and reserve the rest to have later with you and your husband, when you can all sit down together. This is probably not going to be a relaxed meal, because, at best, all you can hope for at this age is about ten minutes of cooperation. But during that time your child can eat his food and you and your husband can talk to him and pay him some attention. Perhaps you can deputize him to help you with the dinner—by setting the table or helping you cook the food—so that he'll feel less left out of the ritual of eating together. During dinner, point out exactly what he did to help you. But make it fast.

If in spite of these measures your child begins to hit either you or your husband, you will have to intervene immediately. Act before he gets out of hand. By now you should be able to see the behavior coming. When you do, interfere with it. Don't let it happen; distract him. You might suddenly, and with some exaggeration, remember something that you forgot to bring to the table and ask him to accompany you to the kitchen to get it. Whatever the distraction is, act swiftly and dramatically to short-circuit the undesirable behavior. If he starts throwing food or hitting you, end the dinner abruptly, tell him that his behavior is unacceptable, remove him to another activity and perhaps wait until he is in bed before you and your husband sit down together again.

Some families plan a meal or two a week without the children. You and your spouse need some time together without the demands and intrusions of your child. Some meals should include him, though, so that he ultimately learns to conduct himself appropriately through practice. His hypersensitivity to being excluded will lessen as he gets older, as will his sense of exclusivity toward each of you. I think it is fairly safe to say that this difficult behavior will pass—but that doesn't mean that you should ignore it while it is in progress.

Masturbation

First and foremost, it's important to realize that masturbation is a normal part of a young child's development. Children as young as eighteen months of age masturbate. It's true for both boys and girls. Sometimes it's simply used as a soothing activity, but at other times children do appear to get excited and worked up. It's obviously a pleasurable experience for them.

Since sexual activities are such a private matter, and since we associate them with adult behavior, it's usually distressing for a parent to see his child engaged in masturbation. In addition, our culture has always disapproved of masturbation, and despite our modern attitudes, we often feel that it's wrong for one reason or another.

Masturbation is not physically dangerous unless the child is doing something hurtful. Girls will either use the hand or will rub up against a pillow or roll up and down on a stuffed animal. Boys will usually use a hand to masturbate.

With this understanding, it should be clear that a child should not be punished or threatened in any way if you notice her masturbating. The first time you notice it, in fact, you needn't say anything at all. It may be just a passing fancy and may not develop into an intrusive habit. For most children, however, masturbation does become a temporary habit during the preschool years. It will last for shorter or longer periods, depending on the child. You may notice that when a child is tired or going to sleep or watching TV, she masturbates to soothe herself. If the child is alone watching TV or listening to music, then there's no need to interfere at all.

If, however, you are involved in an activity with others and the child starts to masturbate, then you should quietly distract her by offering her a drink or something else to do with her hands, which will automatically end the masturbation. If it becomes disturbing to you because it is happening more and more frequently in public, quietly say to the child, "That's something that should be done in private. It's personal. If you want to, you can go into your room. When you are finished you can come out." Try to make the speech as straightforward and matter-of-fact as possible, without instilling any sense of shame or guilt.

Certainly do not use threats to discourage her. I still hear parents tell their children that dreadful things will happen if they continue to masturbate. It is very ill-advised to frighten a child out of the practice. Likewise, punishment for masturbation is not appropriate.

If your child retreats to her room to masturbate, allow her the privacy. Unless you feel that it has become compulsive and is taking excessive amounts of time from other activities, leave her alone. Once in a while you might cheerfully invite her to do something else—something that would occupy her hands. But don't walk in on her if she requests privacy, and don't spy on her. Just forget about it if you can. Masturbation generally ceases to be a concern during the school-age years.

Playing Doctor

The preschool age is a very sexually curious age. These are the years when children will suddenly begin asking questions about where babies come from and will show an exaggerated interest in your body and your nudity. They are also very curious about their peers—about how one sex is different from the other. To satisfy this curiosity, children have developed a game called "playing doctor." All children play this game. Our generation played it. Our parents' generation played it. It's not a new invention. Nor can you stop your children from playing this game. Even if you stop one game in progress, your children will find other places, other times to play it.

So the parent is caught in an odd bind. On the one hand, you can't prevent children from playing games like this. On the other, you can't blithely allow such games to continue in your presence. As a model of civilization—of decorum and restraint—you are obligated to encourage the children to move on to a more socially acceptable activity. But at the same time, you don't want to do this in such a way that you will leave lasting scars or deep shame about sexual curiosity.

If you encounter your child in the act of playing doctor, the best thing to do is to invite the children, without showing any signs that you might be upset, to join you in another activity. Simply ask them to put their clothes on and suggest that they come to the kitchen where they can help you empty the dishwasher or go outside where they can play on a swing set. Do this without conveying the impression that they have done anything wrong. And do not try to fill them with guilt. Your suggestion that they do something else merely means that you think there are more appropriate activities to pursue right now. In other words, you're not forbidding intimacy—but you're not encouraging it, either.

If, however, you come upon your child playing doctor and notice that he and his playmate are harming themselves in some way (children sometimes attempt to put things into their bodies), you should stop the game immediately and explain to the children very clearly that they must not do that. Tell them that bodies are not made for putting toys or other objects into.

As the supervisor of the children's play, you should also try to ascertain if the doctor game was entered into with the same enthusiasm on both sides. If one of the children was coerced into the game, you should explain to your child (and to the other child if it is appropriate) that his body is private and that we all need to respect one another's privacy. In addition, underscore the point that he does not have to allow another person to touch any part of his body. (Exceptions to this, of course, include any caregiver who may bathe or help dress the children.)

Many parents become upset and react too quickly and harshly to childhood sexuality because of their own anxieties. Punishment is not appropriate. It's better to take a reasonable approach toward this essentially normal and healthy part of a preschooler's development.

Bossiness

Between the ages of three and five, children need as many opportunities as possible to interact with other children their age. Up until this time, you and your spouse may have been your child's sole playmates—her best and perhaps only friends. But now she needs to learn how to conform and how to get along with others. It isn't enough for you to tell a child how to do this. You have to give her many chances to practice.

Regardless of whether a child has had lots of playmates before, however, she may become bossy during this stage of development. The reason is not hard to find. For years, she has been pushed around, told what to do and how to behave. She's been almost completely under your command. Suddenly, along with trying on adult roles comes the desire to assert herself more than she ever has. Your child wants to be you—an adult with power and influence—only in her case, to an exaggerated degree. Since she can't very well hope that you will suddenly want to become her slave, she sees play with other children her age as an excellent opportunity to practice her newfound power.

For this reason you will often see a preschooler insist that she be first, the boss or the leader, while the other children present have to be second, the slaves or the followers. This is very common behavior and does not necessarily represent an unhealthy attitude.

You'll also find that your child is bossier at home than she is at a playmate's house or at nursery school. Having others come to play on her own turf enhances her sense of power and leadership. To minimize bouts of bossiness, you might consider arranging play dates at other children's homes. Inquire, after the play date, how the children have done. When your child enters preschool, ask her teacher how well she is able to conform to the rules and regulations. If she conforms at school and is not too bossy at other children's houses, then you shouldn't worry about it too much.

If your child has a special problem with one particular playmate, keep their association to a minimum for a while until she is a little more mature and is able to deal with her urges and impulses. If you are geographically isolated, you will have to make more of an effort to insure that your child has playmates. Don't be tempted to think that your child is better off playing all by herself. Although all children need quiet time to themselves, they also very much need opportunities to practice their social skills. If individual playmates are not available, think about enrolling your child in extracurricular activities such as gymnastics programs, dance lessons or sports to give her a chance to interact with other children her age and to make new friends.

Many parents feel that they should intervene if children are unwilling to share or to play well together. Certainly if the children are hitting each other or pushing each other off a swing set, for example, you should separate them either momentarily or for the day. But if the conflict is merely verbal, give them an opportunity to work it out. Be sure you are there to see that it doesn't escalate into a physical battle.

Later when the children are not feeling so stressed, invite them to participate in an activity with you in which you will all have to take turns and share. As the activity develops, ask the children to suggest ways in which they might share materials or fair ways to take turns. Very often children who battle with each other simply lack knowledge about the many creative ways people can play fairly. By demonstrating how it is done, you encourage their personal resourcefulness and give them a model to emulate later in their play.

Cheating at Games

Almost all preschoolers cheat at games sometime. If you are the parent of a preschool "cheater," take heart in the fact that this behavior is common and usually temporary. Although sticking to the rules may seem sensible to you, that concept isn't terribly binding to a five-year-old. Children this age aren't very good at contracts. To them, something is fair if it goes their way. They will, for the most part, understand that there are rules that govern a game, but they see themselves as exceptions to these rules. They don't mind if *you* play by the rules, but they fully believe that they can change the rules with impunity if they so desire. To them, it's far more important to be first, to win or to make up the moves.

When you play a game with a child, I suggest that you take the role of mentor rather than that of competitor. Play the game not with the intention of winning, but of teaching the child—and even more important, of having a nice conversation together as you play. If you take this approach, you won't have to worry about your own pride when you lose and you won't be so concerned about the proper rules. Although you may begin the game by telling the child the rules, you won't be emotionally invested in keeping to them should your child suddenly have a creative inspiration.

When playing a game with a preschooler, play the game *for* the child. Point out to her that if she makes a certain move she will lose a piece, or that if she moves another way she may be able to take your piece. If your child is about to make a move and you see that the play isn't correct, you can point it out to her. It's very likely, however, that she'll respond by saying, "But I want to move that way." You might try reading to her from the rules.

Once in a while your child may adhere to the rules of an objective third party. On the other hand, she may very well retort, "I don't care what the box says. I know better." In that case, say to her, "Okay, let's take time out from the regular rules and play by your rules for a while." Make it clear that you know hers are not the correct rules.

It's sometimes upsetting to parents to have to play a disorganized game with an illogical set of rules. Orderliness and predictability make us more comfortable. But avoid making threats to end the game if the child doesn't play fairly. Instead, use the opportunity to have an enjoyable interaction, even if you are playing the game in a silly way.

Many parents fear that if they allow their children to make up rules to their own advantage—in other words, to cheat—that they are not doing their job. Won't their children end up cheating at school and in school games as well?

The answer is, probably not. Interestingly, shortly after the age of five, when most children enter first grade, they suddenly become rigid sticklers for rules. Because they are just then beginning to appreciate what a rule is, they become extremely steadfast and often won't hear of bending one, whatever the reason. They also learn, through increased social interaction, to conform better to the group dynamic. For this reason you shouldn't be overly concerned about attempts to cheat in the preschool years.

Lying

Many parents are alarmed and dismayed when they first catch their young children lying. It is disheartening because it suggests a loss of innocence. If a child goes so far as to lie about something she has done, doesn't that mean she knows that what she did is wrong and that she wants to keep you from discovering her wrongdoing?

Yes and no. Children this age live in a magical world—a world of wishes, fantasies and stories. They believe that if they wish a thing to be true hard enough, it may actually be true. Their sense of reality and logic aren't as well grounded as ours. Therefore, if a child does something she ought not to have done and is confronted by her parent, she may wish so hard that she hadn't done it that in her mind, she *didn't* do it.

Let me give you an example. A child was given a piece of candy by her grandmother. The little girl's mother told her that it was okay to have the candy, but that she should not eat it until after dinner. But the little girl, playing alone in her room, couldn't withstand the temptation and ate the candy, inadvertently smearing the chocolate all over her mouth. Her mother, entering her room and seeing the evidence, said, "Did you eat that candy?" The little girl, now fervently wishing she hadn't eaten it—in fact, wishing so hard that she created in her mind a reality in which she hadn't eaten it—said, "No." The little girl told a lie—a ridiculous lie at that—and her mother was upset.

The new reality the girl constructed might have tumbled if her mother had pursued the inquiry and even taken the child into the bathroom to confront the evidence in the mirror. Or it might not have. It can be comical to watch the manner in which a preschooler will defend with all her might a lie she has told—and even become indignant at the thought that her parents could ever suspect her of such a wrongdoing.

In order to be truly responsible for a lie, one has to be aware of purposely distorting reality. But a preschooler's sense of reality isn't as unshakable as that of an adult. Therefore, although small children may not represent the truth as we do, it really isn't fair to call their responses lies.

A preschool child doesn't yet have a well-developed conscience or sense of ethics. You can't hold a youngster without these to being truthful. It's not that your child is a criminal. It's simply that she doesn't yet have a reliable sense of right and wrong. I say *reliable* because she will at times appear to have a keen sense of right and wrong. But she can't depend on it. If the wish to have things go the way she wants them to outweighs her logic, her sense of ethics will disintegrate. Moral judgment develops slowly through different stages.

So what can you do if you catch your child lying? Reprimand her? Or, if your child eats a piece of forbidden candy, but then tells you the truth and says she ate it, do you punish her for the infraction? Or do you reward her for confessing the truth? It's a tricky conundrum.

I think you will find that once you understand your preschooler's moral capabilities at this age—or more to the point, her limitations— your worries about her lying will dissipate. Instead of focusing on the falsehood, deal with the infraction. For example, rather than walking into a child's room and saying rather harshly, "Did you eat that candy?" you might say instead, "Oh, oh, I notice that you ate the candy instead of saving it for after supper, as I asked you to. I guess next time I'll have to hold on to the candy, because the temptation proved too much for you. Want to know how I know you ate the candy? Come with me into the bathroom and I'll show you."

Although your efforts to extract confessions and teach the difference between lying and telling the truth may be futile at this age, I do think you can teach your child many helpful lessons about honesty. In other words, approach the subject from the positive side rather than from the negative.

The best way to do this is to act as a model for honesty yourself. For example, if you find that the grocer has given you too much change, point this out clearly to your child: "Oh, look, the grocer has given me too much change. This money doesn't belong to me. It belongs to him. He would feel terrible if I kept something of his. And it would be wrong of me to keep something that doesn't belong to me, right?"

You might remind your child of some of her own experiences. "Remember when your brother took your crayons into his room and we didn't know where they were, and how bad you felt?" "Remember the time we left your pail and shovel at the beach and we went back to look for them but someone had taken them?" Putting an emphasis on empathy—on caring about how someone feels as a consequence of another's actions—as well as being a model of honesty yourself will do far more toward promoting a child's conscience and a system of ethics than will punishing her for having told a lie.

Later, as we shall see, questions of honesty and morality become much more complex with the many subtle nuances that come into play.

During the grade-school and preteen years, issues regarding public and private moral choices must be addressed. Your handling of this evolving mental process at a young age will provide a foundation for later discussions. For now do not let the untruths slide, but avoid brutal confrontations and harsh punishments.

Name-calling

Although it probably annoys you to be treated disrespectfully when your child calls you a name such as "stupid-head," don't lose your perspective. It is rather amusing in some ways if you consider what mild epithets he is able to muster, after all.

Nevertheless, you should make it very clear to your child in a humane manner that this is not the way you wish to be spoken to. To do this, I suggest that you say to the child, "You are probably mad at me. If you are mad at me, tell me you are mad. I think you can figure out how to tell me, but you may not call me those names. I don't call you names like that."

If it happens again, you will have to be a little more dramatic. This time say to your child, "If you do that again, then I'm afraid I will have to put you in your room. And you will have to stay there for five minutes." Or if you and he are in an interesting place, tell him that if he calls you that name again you and he are going to leave. In other words, give your child a warning and suggest that there will be immediate consequences to his name-calling. It doesn't have to be a big deal—certainly don't make a catastrophe out of it. But the punishment should be fairly swift and humane.

The lesson your child should get out of this exercise is that he may not call you or other people names. Make it clear to him that you don't like being treated that way, and that if he does call you names, you will not be inclined to do something nice for him, and that he will have to leave the play area and be by himself for a while. Expect that your child may have a tantrum or will be fussy and cranky and miserable, and that you and he will probably have a terrible afternoon. You may have a perfectly awful afternoon the next day and the one after that, too, if he calls you names and you stick with your discipline. But if you are consistent, I think you will find that after a day or two, the name-calling will abate. If it recurs, saying "Remember what happens when you do that. Now please stop" may be all that's required.

Don't be tempted to gloss over this issue. You may be able to talk yourself into not minding being called names, but this decision may come back to haunt you in later years. If you let a preschooler speak disrespectfully to you now, you'll have a much harder time of it when your child is a preteen and the issue resurfaces, which it is likely to do then. Lay the groundwork now for a relationship built on mutual respect and your task in the preteen and teenage years will be easier. Besides, a polite but firm defense of your own self-respect is something for your child to emulate.

THE GRADE-SCHOOL YEARS:
MAKING CONTRACTS

When they enter first grade, most children experience a remarkable shift in their personalities. Although there will be transitory regressions, emotional outbursts and episodes of demanding behavior, you'll see your six-year-old move on to a more even keel and show a good deal more maturity than ever before. This greater maturity is the result of age, circumstances in school and the development of logic.

First, let's take a look at your child's emotional development. By the end of his fifth year, a child ideally should have worked his way through the issues of competing with and trying to supplant you. He has been imitating you and identifying with you, and has begun to incorporate a stronger sense of values. Because of this, he now has a better sense of what is expected of him. He may not always be thrilled about what he has to do, but he is able to differentiate between right and wrong in a way that was never before possible for him.

You see in a child this age the beginnings of a sense of what is correct, what is acceptable and what the rules are. As soon as he develops this sense, he can conform to certain rules when he plays a game. He is better able to wait his turn and can cope with the idea of someone else's winning from time to time. Unlike the preschool child, whose self-interest was dominant, the school-age child begins to understand that there are general impersonal regulations that govern him. At first this may cause quite an active inner struggle between his own self-interest and the regulations he now understands exist, which is why this new growth and development is not entirely smooth. One fairly amusing aspect of your child's new comprehension of rules and regulations is that you may find him imposing rigid restrictions upon you! In grappling with the concept of rules and self-discipline, a child may try to discipline those closest to him. He'll want to make the rules, and although he may often see himself as an exception, you may be sure *you'll* have to stick to them.

School also plays a tremendously important part in helping a child this age develop self-discipline and self-control. For the first time, the child is exposed for many hours a day to other people who have rules and regulations and expectations of him. Because he is out there with others, in a classroom with a teacher and a group of students, he will be more likely to conform, less likely to throw his weight around. I think you'll see fewer episodes of negative behavior as well. He may grumble a bit at what the teacher says, but more often than not he will go along with it.

For the first time, your child is beginning to see that other people have rights, too. As a member of a group, he is now expected to participate in group activities, and this helps mitigate the self-importance that governed him through earlier stages. Along with this newfound conformity, you'll probably also notice that he is more concerned with looking like the other children, of doing the same things they do and of belonging to small groups or cliques.

Thrown into situations with other children, your child now has a chance to measure himself against them, to develop the beginnings of an internal yardstick. School also offers him a way to apply his natural potential: All those ideas and all that energy can now be channeled into more productive projects.

With first grade, too, comes the development of such skills as reading, writing, mathematics, recreational activities and crafts. These pursuits, aside from their inherent importance to the child, also play a role in civilizing him. For through them, the child achieves a sense of pride in accomplishing what he sets out to do and develops the concentration and self-discipline necessary to complete the task at hand.

In addition to greater maturity and the changes effected by his entry into grade school, something else very critical is happening to your child. He is developing logic. The logic of the school-age child is very different from the reasoning of the preschool child. At about six years of age, a child begins to have organized mental representations of concepts, whereas the preschool child can't. For example, the preschool child can organize items by putting all the pink blocks in one pile and all the blue blocks in another, and by doing so learn the names of the colors. The school-age child, however, is much better able to juggle those classifications in his mind without needing the actual objects in front of him. He can grasp the concept of blueness or pinkness without having to rely on external examples. This ability to internalize certain ideas leads to the beginning of logical thinking. With logical thinking, he begins to understand the concepts of time and space as adults do.

A school-age child won't be fully comfortable with these concepts until he is ten or eleven, but the formation of logic plays a large part in your relationship with him. Because you and he are beginning to view the world in a similar way, you'll see more compliance and cooperation than you ever have before. There will be less intrusion of magical thinking and fewer episodes of fantasy mixed with reality. You can now begin to give your child rational explanations and expect that they will be attended to. You can also begin to make "contracts" with your child. If he doesn't behave or doesn't fulfill agreed-upon responsibilities, there will be certain specified consequences (grounding or losing privileges). This is the age when a child truly grasps the concept of logically related punishments.

With the child's greater logic also comes a fascination with ritual and organization. As if portraying both Felix Unger and his partner, Oscar Madison, in *The Odd Couple*, the school-age child may vascillate between both sides of his new personality—the ritualistic organized self and the self-interested disorganized self of his earlier years. By the time the child is seven or eight years old, both his logic and his newfound internal controls conspire to put many of those earlier antisocial impulses into place. The desire for ritual becomes even more intense, perhaps as a way of keeping those impulses in check. You'll notice, for example, that your child wants to chant certain songs over and over again and will become a passionate collector. He'll collect stamps, rocks, shells, butterflies, baseball cards, and he'll want them in a particular spot on a particular shelf in his room, and it had better be there!

During the early school-age years, you will also see your child develop what appears to be sexist behavior. Children who played quite happily with playmates of both sexes suddenly want to play only with children of their own sex. In fact, don't be surprised to hear your son say that girls are "disgusting," or vice versa. A child's use of such strong language to describe a group he apparently doesn't want anything to do with (but, of course, he does—witness the way boys and girls chase and taunt each other in the schoolyard) suggests that there may be some fairly intense feelings about the other sex simmering just below the surface. Unable to cope at the moment with these feelings, children turn this unconscious attraction into its opposite, whereby we get the little second grader who "doth protest too much" that girls are "yucky," yet you'll find him in the schoolyard the next day running after the girls and pulling their hair. If he really found nothing of value in the girls, he simply wouldn't bother with them. Instead, his feelings resemble a magnet. One side attracts; the other repels.

Not too long ago I was asked by a second-grade teacher to step in as a kind of "labor negotiator" because the boys weren't getting along with the girls. They were being especially mean to the girls and weren't letting them play on their teams. So I went in very conscientiously to try to help out with the problem. I met with the children in small groups, and then we met as a whole. I worked with certain individuals, and by the end of several weeks, the boys and the girls had agreed on a number of principles. The boys were now willing to let the girls have a turn with the ball. They began to acknowledge that girls were better at some activities than boys. The girls and the boys now had all the right answers, but there was just one problem. It wouldn't stick. Outside school, they went right back to playing just the way they always had.

The reason the intellectual lessons wouldn't stick was that the teacher and I had underestimated the power that came from a desire to belong to a group. Gender group orientation is very important for children this age. It helps them to consolidate the fact that they are boys or girls. It's very confusing for children to deal with both sides of this issue until they are settled within themselves.

Another socializing aspect of grade school is the formation of small groups or clubs or cliques. Children organize themselves into groups; one person is the boss, while others take on various roles within the group. In a sense they are organizing their world as a microcosm of society at large. All of this is good practice in forming relationships outside the immediate family. You'll also see at this age the establishment of "best friends" and, among boys, of chumships, with all the potential for intimacy that these relationships imply.

The grade-school years are a wonderful period of growth and development for most children, but they can also exact a toll. During this period, a child learns to manage his relationships, obey the rules of the school, take instructions from teachers and learn new skills. He's trying to put his best foot forward. But don't be surprised if he comes home and gives you one big difficult time. Sometimes the effort to accomplish all he is trying to do requires that he let loose as soon as he walks in the door. Some children come home from school whining and irritable; others blow up the minute you look at them. Parents, seeing this behavior, sometimes wonder how their child ever survives at school and why the principal hasn't called up threatening to throw him out. Yet it often turns out that the child is a model of good behavior in school. Until he is able to better adapt, however, the cost of behaving well in school may be that he'll be miserable to live with at home.

Throughout all of this growth and development, expect a lot of fluctuation. There will be many ups and downs, although I think you'll see the ups outweighing the downs as time goes on. As your child accomplishes and achieves more, as he controls his own life a bit better and gains a sense of independence, you will find that he is more pleasant to be around. But don't be surprised by the low points—he is still a young child who is quite capable of being cranky and unreasonable.

REALISTIC EXPECTATIONS, PARENTAL GOALS AND TECHNIQUES FOR GRADE-SCHOOL CHILDREN

REALISTIC EXPECTATIONS

1. The child moves onto a more even keel.
2. The child develops logic.
3. The child is able to differentiate between right and wrong in a way never before possible.
4. The child has a better understanding of general and impersonal regulations.
5. The child is better able to conform to a group.
6. The child develops basic learning skills.
7. The child is fascinated with ritual and organization.
8. The child may be subject to emotional fluctuation during this period of growth.

PARENTAL GOALS

1. Encourage your child to take on responsibilities.
2. Encourage self-discipline.
3. Help your child to conform when appropriate.
4. Give your child practice in making judgments.
5. Allow your child to experience the consequences of his actions.
6. Help your child to understand the concept of contracts.
7. Help your child to manage relationships.

TECHNIQUES

1. Investigate the roots of undesirable behavior.
2. Give advance warning of the consequences for unacceptable behavior or unfulfilled responsibilities, and make contracts in which you and your child agree on these consequences.
3. Remove privileges or ground your child if necessary.
4. Be a model for restraint.
5. Have frequent family discussions on issues, problems and values in order to familiarize your child with the democratic process.
6. Use humor whenever possible.
7. Set clear limits.

COMMON PROBLEMS DURING THE GRADE-SCHOOL YEARS

Defiance

General across-the-board defiance from a school-age child will need some investigation to find the roots of the problem. Perhaps you tell your child to come in for breakfast, but she decides instead to get involved in a board game. Perhaps you tell your son to turn off the TV, but he chooses to ignore you and keep watching it. Perhaps your child has become fresh and rude or screams at you whenever you reprimand her or ask her to do a task. In order to curb this behavior, you will first have to find the reason for it.

To do this, a mental checklist is useful: Is your relationship generally rocky? How do you issue your instructions? Is your child tense about something that is unrelated to you, but is using you as a convenient scapegoat? Does your child have problems in school or with a best friend? Does she seem emotionally tense about everything? Do you or your husband ignore or not pay enough attention to your child when she asks you for something? Are you under pressure and having emotional outbursts yourself? Is your child feeling as though you don't give her an opportunity to be independent? Has your discipline been overly punitive lately? Sometimes children are depressed or unhappy, and their non-compliance can be the result of apathy or an effort to expel hidden anger. Defiance is a very complex concept—it can be merely a testing of limits or can suggest deeper psychological difficulties.

If you intuit that your child's defiance is a way of testing the limits you have set for her, be explicit about those limits and tell her that there will be consequences if they are breached. If she should go beyond those limits, make sure you follow through on the consequences. In general it's best for a punishment to be logically tied to the infraction, but if that seems impossible to achieve, then restricting a child's freedom through grounding may be useful. Naturally when you decide to ground a child, it should be for a definite period of time—not open-ended or ambiguous—and it should also be reasonable so that you're not grounding her for a whole season. That would only breed anger. You should also make the grounding realistic: Although recreation may be curtailed, you may want the child to continue other activities such as Girl Scouts or piano lessons during this period. If you find that you have impulsively grounded your child for an excessive length of time, you might consider renegotiating the sentence.

If a child seems to be very uncooperative and verges on being uncontrollable, it may be necessary to think about whether a deeper problem is involved. You should investigate the possibility that the child has either a severe emotional disturbance or a neurological impairment. Children lose control and behave impulsively for many reasons. Sometimes it's anxiety for which the child has no effective means of discharge. A good diagnostic evaluation can help. I suggest a consultation with a pediatric neurologist and a child psychologist to determine the underlying reasons for a child's wild behavior.

Class Clown

When a child acts up in class, you really have to ask why he would want to have others notice him in that way. Many people think that when a child acts up, it's initially to get attention. But clowning behavior rarely begins as an attention-getting device. It actually works the other way around. In an attempt to cope with something he is feeling, a child acts in a certain way and discovers that attention is paid to him as a by-product. Later he may act in a clownish way deliberately because he remembers that it got him noticed—but the first time around, it has to do with more than just wanting attention.

The class clown presents a complex problem. Nobody wants to be seen in an unfavorable light, and most children want only to be accepted and admired. So why would a child want to be seen as a goofball? On the surface, of course, he achieves a level of acceptance and approval by acting up. A child who clowns around in class, pokes fun at the teacher, and manages to say to the teacher all the things the other children may be feeling but are afraid to say will probably take his classmates' laughter as a sign that they approve and accept him for his cleverness. But then, of course, the class can be laughing *at* the clown, rather than with him. And the class can switch its allegiance pretty quickly when the clown gets caught and punished. So even though there may be momentary rewards, the risk of getting into trouble or being laughed at is fairly high. Why would a small child do this? There are a variety of underlying reasons.

First, clowning around can be a cover-up for not knowing the work. A child's quick or smart-alecky response diverts attention from the fact that he simply doesn't know the answer to the academic question. Chronic clowning around, then, can be the child's attempt to cover up the fact that he is unprepared most of the time.

However, sometimes children act the class clown because of emotional troubles at home, which they bring into the classroom in the form of disruptive behavior. Stress or strain in the family, such as marital strife, a separation or illness are emotional distractions that may lead your child to act up in the classroom.

Other children may behave this way because of sibling rivalry at home, which can translate into the school environment. A roomful of classmates is like a roomful of siblings. Conflicts that begin at home may be aired in the classroom by constant fooling around.

Lastly, it should not be overlooked that some children suffer from learning disabilities, attention-deficit disorders or hyperactivity. These problems can contribute to compulsive behavior that looks like clowning around. They may also contribute to academic failure, which can then exacerbate clowning behavior.

In order to stop a child's clowning behavior, parents first need to do a bit of investigating. Attacking the behavior or trying to find the right punishment for it will have little or no effect unless you ferret out and deal with the roots of the problem. If the problem is the child's inability to do the schoolwork, you will have to cope with this issue, perhaps by closely monitoring his work or by hiring a tutor. If the problem is a result of emotional troubles at home, then you will have to help the child deal with the turmoil. Psychological evaluation and counseling may be necessary. If there is no apparent reason for the clowning, I recommend a sensitive examination by the school psychologist to determine whether the child has a behavioral problem or learning disability.

Resist the temptation to control the child or squash his behavior with a series of strict and rigid punishments. Unless you look for the causes of his behavior, imposing a punishment in the hopes of forcing the child to conform may either fail or have serious long-term consequences for his emotional growth and development.

Bedtime

Telling a child when she has to go to bed is a thorny issue. On the one hand, you know that the child needs to get a certain amount of sleep or else she will be a wreck in the morning. On the other, you can't legislate sleep. You can theoretically enforce a bedtime, but you can't make a child fall asleep.

I advocate a reasoning approach. When your child is very tired the morning after she has had a late bedtime, say to her, "I notice you are really tired this morning. Do you realize you didn't fall asleep last night until ten o'clock? I think you need more sleep to feel cheerful and good. Perhaps tonight you might try to go to sleep a little earlier." It's possible that the child hasn't yet made the connection between going to bed at a reasonable time in the evening and waking up feeling good. It's more likely that she does know, but it doesn't hurt to reinforce the idea. Don't nag, but bring it to her attention.

Sometime later in the afternoon, remind her about her schedule and about the tasks she still has left to complete so that she won't be left with too much to do late at night. As her bedtime gets closer, try to eliminate all possible distractions. Share some calm activity with her just before bedtime; keep the room dark and the rest of the house quiet.

If you're really trying to break her of the habit of staying up too late, I advise trying to get her to fall asleep without any distractions whatsoever for at least one week. This includes reading in bed. While I'm not against reading in bed for most children, it sometimes happens that even a sleepy child will force herself to stay awake just so she can get to the next chapter. We're all familiar with this syndrome as adults. The same stimulus to stay awake can also occur with games in bed. A child who is building something sees that if she puts just one more block here, then that will lead to this possible structure . . . and so on.

You might try suggesting to the child that you and she set the alarm for an hour earlier in the morning so that she can read or play then. If she agrees to this, it may help her get onto a different schedule of sleeping and waking.

Be alert to the fact that some children have difficulty falling asleep because they have emotional anxieties or worries. Perhaps you are unaware of something that happened to your child at school or with her friends. To determine if that is the case, sit with her at bedtime and let her empty out the contents of her mind. Put the child at ease, help her to relax, hear her out and offer her some reassurance.

Also keep in mind that children do have different temperaments. One child may rise at the crack of dawn (actually, I get more complaints from parents about that problem), while another child may be what we loosely refer to as a "night" person. There isn't much you can do about these innate body clocks, and at any rate, there's no point in fighting with a child over this issue.

Practicing an Instrument

Extracurricular activities are, for most children, a very good experience. Through them, children can learn valuable skills and can partake of enrichment not otherwise offered by schools. Knowing which activities to choose, however, and how involved you should be as a parent are more delicate matters.

Children at this age are fickle, and it is quite normal for them to want to take one kind of lesson and then suddenly decide to take up something else. While you don't want to encourage such fickleness (nor can you afford it), do try to remain open to change and allow your child some measure of experimentation with different activities.

It's unreasonable to expect that a six- or seven-year-old can intelligently commit herself to years of piano lessons, for example. Perhaps she will discover in a month's time that she really doesn't like the piano. On the other hand, you do want her to give the instrument a fair chance. I suggest that you and your child make a deal: ten lessons on the piano initially with some commitment to practicing, and then if she still enjoys the lessons and the practicing, an extension of the commitment to a longer period of time. It will take many years for her to learn which activities she is good at and which she really enjoys. Expecting her to be able to do that in first grade is not terribly realistic.

Youngsters often have an inflated idea about how quickly they will be able to learn an instrument, and how well they will play. Sometimes they think they'll be playing the piano like Billy Joel in no time, when in fact they need to be prepared for a great deal of hard work. Before you and your child commit yourselves to piano lessons, it's advisable to talk with her about her goals and to give her some idea of what her progress is likely to be. But don't discourage her.

If your child becomes discouraged by her first attempts at a new activity, be supportive. But if it becomes apparent that she really doesn't like the activity, don't force the issue. It's hard to be good at something if you hate it. You don't want to foster a situation in which she slogs away at the lessons merely to please you. This will only cause her stress. If she's not enjoying it, there's little point in continuing. And despite your own disappointment, be careful not to label her a quitter.

Once your child has committed herself to piano lessons and appears to enjoy them, show an interest in her practicing, but don't become a drill sergeant. Of course you will want to encourage her and attend her recitals, and she may even ask for your help on occasion. But don't stand over her as she practices. And don't nag. Let the practicing be her responsibility. If she isn't doing her work, her instructor will tell her soon enough. Let them haggle over it without your interference. Besides, your child may be enjoying the piano entirely at her own pace and according to her own standards. These may not be the same as yours, but your goal is not to create a concert pianist. Rather, it's to allow your child to develop a skill and to have some pleasure while doing so.

Homework

A lot of research now indicates that homework is very useful for children, and that parents can and should get involved. Homework allows a child to learn at his own pace and to go beyond the limits of the class instruction. It can teach self-discipline and may help a youngster develop good study habits. It gives a slower student a chance to catch up if he has missed class work and to compensate for his deficiencies. If homework is not merely busywork, it can improve a child's classroom grades. Yet the question of how involved parents should be is often a tricky one.

A parent should be attentive to the child's homework in such a way that he shows interest and helps the child organize his work and establish good study habits, but a parent should not nag. Be wary of making "as soon as you finish" promises or of telling the child he can't go out to play until he completes his homework. Avoid the language of "rush" and "hurry." In other words, be an ally, not a policeman. Be a party to getting the homework done, but don't take over. If you interfere too much, become too controlling or even do part of the work yourself, the child may get the idea that he's not competent enough to do his own work.

To help your child do his homework and to make it a pleasant experience, show interest in what he is learning. If possible, preview the homework and chat with him about the lessons or tasks. Next, help your child establish a daily schedule. Take care that the time selected for getting the work done isn't as soon as he comes home from school and that you don't pull him out of a game to do the work. But do establish rituals so that the child can study at approximately the same time each day, in the same place. You may also help him plan an order of studying.

I would also suggest dividing up the homework into short intervals, with breaks planned in between so he can stretch his legs or have a snack or a chat with you. Take the time to review homework when it is finished. But resist the temptation to hover over him while he is working. Check it, but don't be overly critical. Praise the work when possible, even if it's something as simple as, "I'm glad you finished that fifteen-minute segment."

Consider being an example for your child by doing your own "homework"—parallel activities during the study hour. Perhaps you could pay bills or do paperwork from your job.

Keep in mind that although you may help your child organize his homework and help in other ways, the responsibility for it has to rest on his shoulders. Say to him, "Look, I'm interested in seeing that you do your homework as you're supposed to. If you don't do it, you won't learn and you won't have important skills. If you fall behind now, it will be harder to cope with future lessons. Let me see if I can help you out."

If you are concerned about a problem with homework, it is sometimes best to wait until the teacher gets in touch with you. You can then discuss with your child the fact that his teacher has some complaints about his work. If you offer your help at that point, he'll see that you are on his side and are not a collaborator with the "enemy."

Don't try to accomplish everything at once. Concentrate on one subject at a time, or on one time segment. You can build on the small successes gradually. Encourage your child to explain some of the new things he is learning. In this way, he may attempt to master the material in order to discuss it with you. And remember, homework is a terrific way to begin independence training.

Cleaning His Room

Requiring your grade-school child to clean his room is tough because many other activities will compete for his attention, and you can be sure that keeping his room tidy will come dead last. Although I believe that a child should have some authority over the privacy of his own room— over what and who goes into it—I do think you can point out to him that because the room is part of the house, it is part of the family community, just as the family belongs to a larger community. As part of this larger community, you cannot, for example, throw your garbage out the window. Similarly, your child will have to conform to certain basic standards of neatness within the family community. When and how this work gets done, however, is something the two of you will have to negotiate.

This process can be done somewhat democratically, even though I don't believe that families with small children are democratic units. Not everybody in the family is an equal voter or an equal partner. Children are not as experienced and as informed as their parents are. In this area, however, I suggest that you try a little democratic negotiation. The family is a good training ground for democratic procedures.

Tell your child that you would like to have a discussion about the maintenance of his room. Explain that you don't mean by this that he has to scrub the floors or wash the windows or polish the furniture, but that there are certain basic tasks that need to be done.

Ask him what he thinks he should do in his room to maintain a minimum level of neatness. If he says nothing, then respond that you have a different opinion. If he names ten or twelve chores, suggest that perhaps that's too much and that you don't think he'll be able to handle it.

After you have talked for a bit, decide together what the basic chores ought to be. Perhaps he has to put his toys away and make his bed. Possibly you will decide that the bed should be made every day, but that the toys need be put away only once a week. Talk about what time of day the bed should be made by, and what day of the week would be best to put the toys away.

Once you have made these decisions, you can't then nag your child all day. Agree on a time by which the appointed tasks must be done. I suggest writing out a sign that you can put in his room on the agreed-upon day that says, "This is clean-up day." For example, have on the sign a reminder that the bed has to be made by 9:00 A.M. (as it does every day), and that the toys have to be put away by 8:00 P.M.

Now what happens if your child doesn't clean up his room under the rules to which you have both just agreed? Anticipating that this might at some time be the case, ask him during your initial discussion to suggest an appropriate consequence if he doesn't clean up his room. See what he comes up with. Perhaps he will suggest that you ground him, or that you temporarily take away a privilege. Whatever he decides, if it sounds reasonable, say, "Okay, that's the deal," and shake his hand. And then follow through on it if he doesn't meet his end of the bargain.

Allowance and Money Management

One concern parents frequently have is the age at which they should introduce their child to the concept of managing money. It's good to begin this in the toddler and preschool years—by letting a small child handle money and give it to the cashier or the bus driver when appropriate, or by giving a child a piggy bank to watch coins grow into a bigger pile—but it is really in the grade-school years that a child can benefit most from an allowance and from lessons on money management.

Some parents feel that their child has to earn his allowance. I would qualify this, however. Although I feel that a child should perform chores because he is a member of the family, I do not think that having small amounts of money should be contingent upon completing tasks. When you think about it, children really have nothing of their own. They are totally dependent upon what we give them. Because of this, it's useful for a child to have a certain amount of money of his own every week. Having this money helps him learn to make decisions. It's his money, and he can choose what to do with it himself. If he makes a poor choice, it's his mistake and he will learn from it. That doesn't mean that you

have no role in guiding your child. Certainly you can offer suggestions if
you think his choice is an unwise investment or if he is about to buy
something unsafe.

To determine the proper size of the allowance, find out what the
going rate is in your area and see if you can afford it. You may review
with your child what the allowance is going to cover. It's my feeling that
the child should not be expected to pay for necessities such as transportation, milk at school or lessons out of his allowance. An allowance
should be weekly money that you give your child for discretionary purposes—money for a toy, the movies or extra treats at lunch or after
school.

Suppose your child spends all his allowance the first day and has
nothing left. Should you then come to his rescue? The first time this
happens, you might extend him a loan or an advance on next week's
allowance, pointing out that if he spends all his money or budgets un-
wisely, he may be left without funds when he really wants them. Say to
the child, "You spent both your quarters. Now you have none left. I'll
give you a little more this time, but remember that if you spend all your
money, you won't have any at the end of the week." Next time, don't
offer to give the child extra money. Simply remind him, without tortur-
ing him about it, that he needs to learn to budget more wisely.

It's important when teaching your child about money to keep a proper
perspective. Obviously you want to convey to him that money isn't
everything. Money can be a very emotional issue and often is used as a
substitute for love or as a power base. For this reason, don't use money
as a bribe, a reward or in the service of punishing the child. If you use
money as an incentive, a child may begin to identify money with love,
approval, obedience and power. I have nothing against buying a child a
present as a reward on occasion, but don't make a habit of it. Likewise,
if a child is disobedient, taking away a week's allowance isn't going to
make the problem disappear.

Recently a mother called me to say that her son had been doing
poorly in school. At the same time, he'd been talking about buying
himself a particular model airplane with money he had saved out of his
allowance. The woman's ex-husband said that he didn't think the child
should be rewarded after doing poorly in school, and he didn't want the
boy to have the plane. My reaction to that was, what does buying himself a model airplane have to do with poor grades? Moreover, there really
is no question of reward or punishment, because the child was buying a
toy with his own money. Once you give a child money, it is no longer

yours. It becomes his to do with as he pleases. To give a child money and then insist that it come under your control as a reward or punishment is a terrible disservice. It renders a child powerless and defeats the purpose of teaching him self-management.

During the grade-school years, a child can be introduced to the concept of finance as well as allowance. Even as early as first grade, you can offer the child an opportunity to open a bank account to teach him about savings and interest. I also think it's a good idea for a child to have some knowledge about the family finances. If you are buying a new car, let them hear your thoughts. Compare the value of various models and discuss the methods of financing. If you are thinking of purchasing other large items, such as a vacation, allow the child to hear how much it costs. All of this helps him learn about decision making, about setting priorities, about making choices and about knowing that it isn't possible to have everything you want when you want it. If there are financial problems, don't hide them from the child. Without scaring him, make him aware that money is temporarily tight and that the whole family will be making efforts to cut costs.

The best model for a child regarding money is yourself. To do this, set an example for restraint. Explain to your child what things cost, teach him about comparison shopping, introduce him to sales, teach him to read labels and help him to evaluate advertising claims. Then with your guidance, let him practice making money decisions for himself.

Television

Television has a tremendous impact on a child, both in terms of how many hours a week he watches and of what exactly he sees. If you are concerned about the effects TV has on your child, you need to think about many issues: what television offers a child, how many hours a week are suitable for him to spend watching it, the violence and suggestive sex on some shows and the commercial messages aimed at children.

In addition, you should spend some time thinking about the role television plays in your family as a whole: Is the TV set a central piece of furniture in your home? Is it on during the daytime? Is it part of the background noise of family life? Are you yourself addicted to TV? You can try to regulate the subject matter of the shows and limit the number of hours of TV your child watches, but if television plays a central role in your family life, this task will be considerably harder. We are told that the average American child watches twenty-seven hours of TV per week.

That's almost four hours per day. With that kind of national average, I think television watching is an issue that more families ought to be grappling with.

Television is a medium for communication—a neutral medium that can be used any way we want. Chiefly, television provides us with entertainment and information. Critics of television point out that the information we get from it is incomplete by virtue of programming contingencies—news stories can't be covered as fully as they are in print—and that the entertainment is not as culturally advanced as it might be. These issues are matters that parents can and ought to evaluate for themselves.

By now, everybody knows that there is a lot of violence on television. Even if we disagree on the impact such violence has on a child's behavior, most of us would agree that it's not wonderful for a child to be exposed constantly, several hours a day, day after day, week after week, to televised violence. According to the American Psychological Association, research has shown that such exposure has at least these three effects: children may become less sensitive to the pain and suffering of others; they may become more apprehensive of the world around them; and they may be more likely to behave in an aggressive manner toward other people. I would add a fourth possible effect: I think televised violence gives children a disproportionate sense of the amount of true violence that exists in the world.

Violence isn't the only troubling theme on many TV shows. Parents ought to think long and hard about the daytime or evening programs in which people are engaged in suggestive sexual activities or are pouring drinks for themselves. A nine-year-old boy doesn't need to see portrayals of fairly explicit sex on TV, nor does he benefit in any way from seeing alcohol use portrayed as socially acceptable or fun.

Violence, sex and addictive behavior are themes that a parent ought to be wary of when regulating a child's TV watching, but even if the material shown on television were uniformly excellent for children, the issue of quantity would be an important one. Obviously, if a child invests a certain number of hours per week watching television, that leaves fewer hours for other activities—ice-skating, dance lessons, painting, music lessons, gymnastics, socializing with friends, reading, working on a computer, drawing, writing short stories, working with wood, making up games, fantasy activities or just going for a walk. If your child is watching upwards of twenty hours per week of television, when will he ever have time for these other pursuits—particularly when you consider that school, homework, a few chores, eating and sleeping take up a lot of time themselves?

Parents should manage television much the same way you would manage the other aspects of your child's life. How much junk food do you permit your child to eat? How much exercise do you want your child to get? What safety precautions do you take when your child is traveling alone? Personally, I don't think children should watch more than one hour of television a day. Nor do I think there is anything wrong with saying to a child on some nights that he can't watch any television at all. In fact, if you can get away with it, you might try to prohibit TV watching on school nights. This may be hard to do, and I don't think you can rule out television completely; it's become too much a part of our culture. And I'm not sure that ruling it out altogether would be to the child's advantage. Children, including preschoolers, can and do benefit from watching certain informative, educational programs.

One of the most important caveats about TV watching is that it shouldn't become a habit. Rather, television viewing should be a finite activity, one with a beginning and an end, much like playing a game or painting a picture. If possible, get a portable TV that you can bring out for a specific show and then put away, just as you would put away books or painting materials.

When your child is watching his one hour per day of TV, sit down with him if you can and comment occasionally on what is happening in the show. If the show has some violent scenes, interject your own values and comments: "That guy really didn't have to shoot the other one. Isn't that a horrible way to have to settle a dispute?" Doing this helps mitigate the intensity of the child's involvement with the violence. You can also help your child distance himself from the violence by pointing out that one fellow didn't really hit the other, that there are ways of staging such scenes, and that the blood is really just one of a number of intriguing special effects.

I wouldn't be above brainwashing your child about which shows you think are good and which you think are just awful. Nor would I hesitate to enlighten a child about products that are advertised on TV. If you watch a commercial with your child, say to him, "Remember when we saw that toy at the store and it was just a piece of junk? You can't always tell when you see it on TV, because there are ways of filming it at different angles to make it look bigger and more powerful. Keep that in mind when you think you want all those toys they advertise."

The best model for restraint when it comes to television is yourself. If you and your spouse are TV addicts, if the TV is on most of the day as background noise or blaring away while you're putting your child to bed, any efforts at governing your child's TV watching are going to be considerably more difficult.

Greed

Greed is an unattractive quality in any person, but it can be especially distressing to see in young children. Yet children *can* become greedy, particularly around holiday seasons or birthdays. With all the excitement and anticipation surrounding these occasions, it's the rare child who remains uninvolved. When children are bombarded with commercial messages, it's even more difficult to remain aloof.

Children think that their wishes will be automatically fulfilled, and the advertisements on TV do nothing to disabuse them of this notion. Sometimes the wish for toys fills up a need for something lacking in their lives, whether that need is real or imagined. In addition, in a child's mind a gift is often equated with love. This notion is reinforced by commercial messages that imply that the bigger and better the gift, the more the child is loved by his parents.

Some excitement and anticipation is natural, but if it threatens to get out of hand in your household, deal with the matter by having a family discussion. Talk with your child about the intangible pleasures of the holiday season—the meaning behind the celebration, the age-old family traditions you'll all be experiencing, the baking, the singing, the making of gifts for others. Point out that there are some very good things about the holidays besides the presents he will be getting. You shouldn't expect that this "brainwashing" will sink in entirely, but it may take the edge off his greed.

As the holidays grow closer, engage your child in some of the activities you discussed with him so that he can experience them firsthand. Make a list with him of presents he can make or buy for other people, let him bake holiday cookies with you, and let him get involved in the rituals and traditions.

Make intelligent decisions about what you can afford for your child or what you think best for him, and don't give in to his requests or demands if he asks for something you either cannot afford or don't think appropriate. You may be tempted to give in because you don't want him to be disappointed when he opens his presents, but learning to cope with disappointment is part of growing up, too.

Also be careful not to connect demands for good behavior with holiday gifts. During the holiday season or prior to a birthday, many harried parents use presents as bribes or threaten to take away presents unless their children behave. This tactic, however, is really a form of blackmail and reinforces the material aspects of your relationship.

The best way to teach a child restraint and generosity is to be a model of those qualities yourself. If your child sees that you want a particular item but refrain from buying it, either because it isn't practical or because you can't afford it, he will begin to understand restraint. Likewise, if you donate books or clothing to charity, take him with you to distribute the items to teach him about generosity.

Learning self-control won't happen overnight. Nor will appreciating the less tangible signs of love. These are parts of a lifelong maturing process. Right now is an excellent time to start.

Table Manners and Politeness

Parents shouldn't be too strict about table manners, because it takes the joy out of eating for youngsters. This is one of those cases where parents have to put their expectations in line with the child's capabilities and needs, and not be swayed by the traditional expectations of a generation ago, when the dinner hour was thought to be sacred and an occasion for lessons on manners as well as on morals.

First off, it's important to make a distinction between at-home table manners and public manners. If you think about it for a moment, I'm sure you'll agree that your own at-home manners are different from those in a restaurant or at a dinner party. Don't you sometimes pick at the bread or the turkey before you bring it to the table? Don't you sometimes serve yourself first at home?

Make it clear to your child that some table manners are not acceptable in public, whereas they might be at home—and that certain behaviors are not acceptable anywhere. Children shouldn't touch food that other people have to share, they shouldn't put their fingers in the butter, and they shouldn't handle every piece of bread before they select the one they want. If your child is chewing with her mouth open—something children may do unconsciously—and people find it disturbing, call it to the child's attention in a nice way. "Try to remember to chew with your mouth closed, because people don't like hearing other people chew," you might say, but do not humiliate the child, and don't badger her.

You may find you're making a mistake in trying to keep your child at the table long after she has finished her own meal while you and your spouse finish yours. Young children find it very difficult to sit idly for long periods and I think it's counterproductive to force a child to sit through a meal like an adult. When your child finishes her dinner, let her go play with her toys or work on her homework or do whatever she can do by herself. It's fine to want to have a family conversation during the dinner hour if you can manage it—I just don't think you ought to prolong it beyond the point at which your child has finished her meal.

Manners don't end at the dinner table. A certain amount of decorum and respect should be taught by promulgating decent manners in many areas of social life—traveling in trains, buses and planes; when guests come to the house; and in dealings with other adults, such as in stores or supermarkets. When I'm in an elevator, for example, and a person pushes in front of me, I feel offended. I think we're all particularly sensitive when we see young people behaving in a thoughtless, rude manner.

Even though on any given occasion your child may be impatient, say to him, "Let Mr. Smith pass first." Being able to do so conveys not only self-control but also respect for another person simply because he or she is older. Similarly, on public conveyances, you might suggest to your child that he offer to hold a door or lift a suitcase or give up his seat to an elderly person. Of course, if you demonstrate this kind of behavior yourself, your child will be more likely to do so, too.

When guests come to the house, your child should greet them in a polite manner. If a friend or relative comes to visit and your child balks at the greeting or acts sassy, you might tell him, after the guest has left, that he hurt the guest's feelings, that the guest was only trying to be friendly, and that he behaved disrespectfully.

Whether a child should respond to greetings from strangers depends on the age of the child. Certainly I would not expect a three-year-old to return a stranger's greeting in the supermarket—especially in this era of concern about strangers and children. An older child, however, can return a greeting in a polite fashion without encouraging further conversation if he doesn't want to—but he will need you and your good manners to show him how to do this.

School Refusal

Some children can't wait to go to school. Others seem to have an unusual degree of fear or avoidance attached to school. School refusal, or school phobia, as it is sometimes called, has a number of possible origins, and your most urgent priority will be to find out exactly what is causing the problem.

First, try to find out if the issue is fear of school or fear of leaving home. The two matters are quite different. In the first case, there may be something at the school itself—fear of failing, fear of being teased, fear of riding the school bus—that is bothering your child. In the second case, the child may be afraid to leave home because she thinks something bad may happen in her absence. For example, if you have recently brought a new baby into the family, your older child may not want to leave home for fear that her absence may cause you to grow closer to the baby. Or if you and your spouse have been fighting a lot lately, she may be afraid that something drastic, such as a separation, will occur while she's not there.

Talk with your child to ferret out the source of her concern and help allay her fears. If you discover in the course of your discussion that other children are teasing her or that she is anxious about the work she is expected to do, suggest ways of dealing with the problem. If, on the other hand, you determine that the cause of her anxiety is stress at home, reassure her that nothing untoward will happen in her absence.

It is sometimes helpful to arrange for play dates at your home with some children from the class. That way, your child will have friends to see when she goes off to school. You might also consider being class mother, or going along on class trips.

Some parents have discovered that their child's fears are lessened if she takes something of theirs to school with her—a photograph or a set of keys, perhaps. The token seems to comfort a child. Each day after school, be sure to tell your child how proud you are of her for sticking it out.

Most children will settle down after a short time. Ask the teacher each day how much your child was able to participate. If that amount increases daily, even if the increments are small, then I think you needn't worry. You can expect that your child will complain the next day and the next, but I think you'll see, fairly shortly, that she'll be able to make the adjustment. If, however, the fear persists for more than two or three weeks, I would advise that you have your child evaluated by the school psychologist to determine if she has a more serious emotional problem.

Wetting the Bed

A child who is a bed wetter is probably just as distressed about the problem as you are. He may not have to change the sheets, but in all likelihood, it curtails his social life. Going to a sleep-over at someone's house or having another little boy to come sleep at your place are probably out of the question for him because of the bed-wetting. Your child is likely to be anxious about his problem, and it interferes with all sorts of activities, not the least of which may be falling asleep at night because he is afraid he will wet the bed if he loses consciousness.

There are many causes of bed-wetting, some of which we are just beginning to understand. First, check with your pediatrician to be sure there is nothing medically wrong. I would also advise that your child be seen by an allergist, preferably a pediatric allergist. Some specialists seem to think—although the data are still controversial—that bed-wetting may be related to what the child eats. Milk products may play a role in bed-wetting, for example. Although allergies may not be the cause of your child's bed-wetting, it's helpful to be able to rule them out.

Some children who have been dry for a time and then start to wet the bed again may do so because of emotional stress. Perhaps a new baby has been born, perhaps someone is sick, perhaps you have moved. These factors can cause children to regress and to wet the bed. Usually parents will notice a pattern—the child wets the bed when he is under stress, and when the stress is removed, the bed-wetting goes away.

Another prevalent theory about bed-wetting is that it is a sleep disorder. When moving through the various stages of sleep, some children empty their bladders without waking. This behavior is beyond their control. Such bed-wetting may be dealt with by having a pediatrician prescribe certain drugs that change the child's level of sleep and allow him to wake up at the sensation of a full bladder. One of the problems of using such drugs, however, is that when the child is taken off them, the bed-wetting may recur. You must also be mindful of potential side effects of medication. Sleep-disorder bed-wetting may continue until the child is in his teens, and the tendency is thought to run in families. If one parent was a bed wetter, this increases the likelihood that the child will be one. And if both parents were bed wetters, the chances are even greater.

Certain kinds of liquids may play a part in bed-wetting. Fluids containing caffeine, for example, are thought to stimulate the bladder and may lead to more frequent urination. To determine if this is the cause of your child's bed wetting, eliminate foods and liquids from his diet that contain caffeine, such as some sodas and chocolate.

There are also several mechanical devices that may help train a child to wake up when his bladder is full. One is a rubber sheet wired with a bell that goes off when the child first starts to wet, waking him up before he has fully urinated in the bed so that he may finish in the toilet. The idea behind this device is for the child to learn gradually, by anticipating the bell in his sleep, not to urinate at all until he gets into the bathroom. This technique is advisable only for fully toilet-trained children over the age of six. I would not subject a small child who is just learning to stay dry during the night to this kind of stress.

It is also possible to help your child increase his bladder control in these ways: During the day, have him stop and start the stream of urine once it is in progress. Also, ask him to delay urinating for a moment when he has the urge. This is very difficult for a child to learn, but once mastered, it may help.

What should be clear here is that bed-wetting is *not* an occasion for punishment. Your child is not wetting the bed because he is naughty. In fact, bed-wetting is something over which he has virtually no control. Forcing him to wash his sheets and pajamas or shaming him is cruel and useless. To solve the problem, you first have to determine the cause —either through your own investigations or with the help of specialists —and then offer your child whatever assistance is necessary to stop the problem. Be reassuring, too. Tell your child that he will eventually have dry nights and that it is only a matter of time.

THE PRETEEN YEARS:
REINFORCING VALUES

Some children begin to shift gears around the age of ten or eleven and enter what we have come to call the preteen years. Changes in attitude, behavior, thinking and personality mark this stage of development, but the age at which a child will enter this phase is not as clear-cut as it was for earlier stages of growth. In fact, all the previously discussed issues pertaining to the school-age child continue to be in effect. In a sense, then, the term preteen is an arbitrary one. The picture is further confused by the fact that boys and girls do not appear to experience the preteen years in exactly the same way at exactly the same time. For the most part, girls this age will seem more sophisticated in their thinking and in their concerns than boys.

In many respects, the preteen years mimic adolescence, but without one essential ingredient: hormones. Most ten- and eleven-year-olds have not yet experienced puberty—but this milestone is not far below the horizon. Some children this age eagerly await puberty. Others are anxious about its onset. And still others are more or less oblivious to the entire issue until it hits them. By the time a child has reached the preteen years, however, he should have had from his parents a substantial education in sexual matters so that he will be prepared for what is to come and won't be frightened or startled by the physical signs of maturity when they arrive.

Even without the real stuff of the teenage years (those hormones) you will notice that your child becomes more involved with the expression of feelings. During this period, for example, some girls may begin to keep detailed diaries, writing in them their innermost thoughts and sometimes sharing these thoughts with close girlfriends. Other children will suddenly become moody, mimicking the roller-coaster highs and lows that you'll see in extreme form during the teenage years. Others may become irritable and angry, testing and challenging you on what would appear to be very minor issues and often showing an exaggerated sense of injury when their feelings are hurt.

Some of this emphasis on feelings is due to a new development in the child's mental capabilities. In the school-age years, we saw the beginnings of logic. Now we observe not only a deepening of emotions, but the growth of abstract reasoning. This is not quite the true abstract reasoning ability that will come to fruition during adolescence, but it is a step in that direction. During the preteen years, your child may find himself caught in a transition period between the more concrete thinking of the school-age years and the abstract reasoning of the teen years. This will undoubtedly confound him as well as you on occasion.

You will begin to see your child's burgeoning abstract thinking in the way he is now able to formulate hypothetical situations for your contemplation, and also in the way he develops counterarguments to yours. You now have to be responsive to a different kind of mental process in your child, and this can sometimes be very unnerving. Knowing that this is but a mild foreshadowing of the extreme testing you will face during your child's teen years may not be very comforting, but it may be useful to look upon the preteen years as good practice for the hard stuff later. These are also good years for you and your child to work on developing negotiating skills, and for you to make a concerted effort to instill in your child the values you think are vital and worthwhile. Be aware that you will continue to have quite a bit of control over your child: A ten-year-old is still pretty dependent upon his family, emotionally, socially and physically.

Much of your preteen child's new abstract thinking will be put into play in the service of breaking away from you. Although more vigorous attempts to separate from you won't come until a few years later, you will almost certainly begin to observe a kind of awkward push-pull in your relationship.

You may find yourself the target of a great deal of bickering and badgering with your eleven-year-old as he prepares for independence. In order to break away from you, it is necessary for him to find fault with you. It's very hard to separate from someone you think is perfect or on whom you depend for everything. Your child will be discovering new areas of independence that may come into conflict with previous attitudes and ways of doing things in your household. Just realizing the roots of this bickering or faultfinding may help you tolerate it. While you should not allow your child to be disrespectful toward you, I think you will shortly discover that you are going to have to listen to a lot more differences of opinion than you have been used to.

One of the phrases that you may hear a lot during these years is "Don't you trust me?" This expression doesn't seem to come up earlier, but many parents of preteens find that it surfaces during this stage of development. The phrase is a particularly interesting one because it combines so many of the issues confronting the preteen: the development of abstract reasoning, the deepening of feelings and the push-pull preparations for independence. The phrase also tends to be a conversation stopper. Many parents are startled when they first hear it, and are often baffled as to how to respond. Let me give you an example.

An eleven-year-old boy wasn't doing his homework. His grades were beginning to fall. His father wanted to encourage the boy to try harder and to do his work. One evening he sat down with the boy and had a talk with him about his homework. "I can handle it myself," said the boy. "Yes," the father answered, "except that you're not." "But I can," insisted the boy. "Well, I would like to help you," said the father, "because it looks as if your grades are falling behind."

Suddenly the boy stood up. "Don't you trust me?" he said, full of indignation.

The father was thrown off balance. Of course he trusted his son. But then again, he didn't trust his son to do his homework. The issue was suddenly more complex than any he had ever encountered in child rearing before. His son was confusing a formerly straightforward issue with abstract thinking. To the father's credit, he answered his son, "Yes, I trust you in most matters, but this is an area where I think you may need some of my help. And I'm not sure that trust is the issue here. The facts speak for themselves. You are not doing the work. Your grades are falling."

The way a child will bring abstract reasoning to bear in his relationship with you also ties in with another typical preteen issue: As a parent, do you allow your child to live with the consequences of his actions and judgments, or do you step in and make his decisions for him?

During the school-age years, a child who is given practice at decision making has an opportunity to make some judgments for himself. But because he is still so young, the matters his parents allow him to decide are probably not terribly critical. As the child grows older, however, and enters the preteen years, the situations that come up for judgment are more complex and have more serious consequences. Deciding when to let a child live with these consequences can be a very delicate matter.

In the example mentioned above, the father might have allowed his son to live with the consequences of poorly done homework for the first marking period of seventh grade to let him learn firsthand what happens if he doesn't do the work—but he might not want his son to fall too far behind, lest the matter get out of hand. Letting a child slip up on his homework during his senior year in high school is a different matter from teaching the son a painful lesson in the seventh grade.

Because of the more difficult nature of the issues you will face as the parent of a preteen, you will find that your judgment is often strenuously exercised. Resist the temptation, however, to be too controlling of your child's behavior during this phase. Without the opportunity to make mistakes, to try and fail, a child cannot build the foundations for good judgment that will be so vital later on.

Preteens are sometimes deceptive. Because they can appear to be quite sophisticated and self-assured and can resemble teenagers in their gestures and dress, we might be tempted to ascribe to them a level of maturity they don't yet possess. They still require tremendous parental support. Your task as a parent is to guide your preteen through this phase with moderation and flexibility. Too much freedom can result in physical and emotional risk; too-restrictive handling can engender rebellion.

Despite the ups and downs that may occur, this phase of child rearing is rewarding. Youngsters show industriousness as well as an appreciation for others. Their talents and interests burgeon, a weird sense of humor becomes apparent and their social awareness expands. It is actually quite a nice age.

REALISTIC EXPECTATIONS, PARENTAL GOALS AND TECHNIQUES FOR PRETEENS

REALISTIC EXPECTATIONS

1. Behavior may mimic adolescence.
2. Girls may be more mature in their thinking and in their concerns than boys.
3. Both boys and girls may be moody and involved with the expression of feelings.
4. The preteen exhibits the growth of abstract logic.
5. The preteen may exhibit beginning attempts to break away.
6. A sense of ethics should be well developed.
7. Peer pressure may be more potent than loyalty to the family.

PARENTAL GOALS

1. Make sure your child has had a substantial education in sexual matters.
2. Develop negotiating skills.
3. Help your child develop good judgment and civic responsibility.
4. Protect your child's physical and emotional health.

TECHNIQUES

1. Handle sensitive matters delicately. Try to avoid very harsh punishments and empty threats.
2. Provide clear guidelines for sexual and social conduct.
3. Be a model for restraint and civilization.
4. Provide ample education regarding dangers of drugs, alcohol and smoking.
5. Give your child handy excuses to withstand peer pressure so he can avoid drugs, alcohol and smoking.
6. Give your child opportunities for making judgments.
7. Make it clear that you will not condone cheating, lying, stealing, vandalism, rude and fresh behavior or the taking of drugs, alcohol or tobacco.
8. Allow your child to experience logically related punishments; if those are impossible, then make it clear that privileges will be removed or the child will be grounded for infractions.

9. Make limits clear.
10. Take your child's opinions seriously. Do not patronize a competing viewpoint.

COMMON PROBLEMS WITH PRETEENS

Being Fresh and Talking Back

Children are occasionally rude during the preschool age. This issue is very likely to surface during the preteen phase as well and may set the tone for your forthcoming relationship during the difficult teenage years if it's not nipped in the bud.

Quite often, preteens are not rude when they are alone with their parents, but they are rude in front of their friends. Preteens usually consider the peer group much more important than parents. A child this age may feel that she would rather be with her friends, that she doesn't really care what her mother or father thinks, and that she would just as soon live without them. The fact that this, of course, is not entirely practical doesn't necessarily change the way she feels when her acceptance by the peer group becomes paramount.

You want your child's loyalty to be to you, but chances are that when she is around her friends she feels allegiance to them. She does not want them to see her as being babyish in any way, nor does she want to lose their support and acceptance. In many ways she thinks she is better understood by her peers than by you, and sometimes this is true. Much of your job is to impose a value system upon your child—but that doesn't always give her the comfort she is looking for. It's sometimes easier to go along with friends who can see things from the same point of view as she and who have the same kind of judgment.

When a child gives you a fresh answer, implied in that answer is her attempt to preserve an image and to save face. She wants to show her friends how independent she is and that she doesn't have to take anything from anybody—least of all, you. Ideally she would like to demonstrate that she has no restrictions; preteens frequently engage in a kind of competition over such matters as who has the latest curfew or who can watch which television program. Being fresh to you may be her crude way of demonstrating her imagined maturity.

You can avoid that confrontation altogether if you are careful not to play to an audience—and not to let her do the same. If you reprimand your child in front of her friends, she may feel it necessary to try to hold her own, regardless of the consequences to you and later to herself. If, for example, she is playing in her room with her friends and has forgotten to go get her brother next door as you asked her to do, don't just barge into her room and issue a command. Rather, call her outside and remind her, confidentially, that she was supposed to get her brother. That way you avoid the possibility that she will be fresh to you to save face in front of her friends.

When she *is* fresh to you, avoid a public confrontation. She will almost certainly retaliate, causing you to retaliate further. The moment the offense occurs, simply say, "I'm not going to dignify that with an answer. I don't want you to speak to me that way." Then cut off all conversation.

Later when the two of you are alone, say to her, "I'd like to have a few words with you." Be very serious; take the child into a private area and sit down. She won't want to look at you and she won't want to hear what you have to say. But you must insist that she stay and listen to you. Make it short and to the point. Tell her first that you will not tolerate her calling you a name. Say it very seriously: "Don't ever speak to me that way again. That's not how I am to be addressed." Second, point out to her how unbecoming it is when she says those words. "Do you know what you sound like and how you look when you say things like that to me?" First you will have made it clear that you absolutely won't stand for that kind of disrespect, and second, that such behavior has tarnished her image in your eyes. Anger can be expressed in constructive ways, but rudeness is to be discouraged.

Next you should discuss the consequences of her speaking to you like that again. Try to avoid suggesting that she will not be allowed ever to have her friends over, because it will almost certainly turn out to be an empty threat, and in the end you will lose face over it. I'm sure such a punishment would not help very much anyway. The consequences should be more immediate.

Make it clear to your child that if she continues to call you names or to treat you disrespectfully, you will deprive her of something she wants in the near future. Don't punish her retroactively, but do tell her that if she behaves badly again, she will miss out on a certain privilege. Also point out *why* she will be missing out on the privilege: "If you can't be considerate of me, then I am not going to put myself out for you. You wanted to go ice-skating on Saturday? Well, if you call me a name, you won't be allowed to go. You've already paid your money? Well, I don't care. I won't be blackmailed. These are the consequences if you are disrespectful to me."

Or perhaps she had planned a sleep-over party on the weekend with her friends. "You wanted your friends over on Saturday? If you don't treat me with respect and consideration and you won't go along with what I am asking of you, then I am certainly not going to allow you to have your friends over." Your daughter may then complain that she's already invited everybody. "Fine," you should say. "If need be, you may have to uninvite them."

The point is to make your child feel the consequences of her disrespect to you immediately. Spell out to her exactly what will happen if she continues to treat you in that unpleasant manner. If she then speaks rudely to you or gives you some lip, follow through with the punishment. In the long run, I believe that your child will have more respect for you if you handle the matter justly and without ambivalence. I don't mean that she will merely show you respect, but that she will feel it. She will understand that your feelings matter. Moreover, by demonstrating that you have self-respect and are willing to stand up for it, she will appreciate your viewpoint. It also serves as a model for her. It's to be hoped that she, in turn, will expect civility from others and will be offered the appropriate respect.

Telephone Use

It can be very frustrating to have a preteen in a home with only one telephone line. During these years, children are much more apt to be on the phone with their friends than they were in earlier years because they are becoming increasingly social and involved in "business." They have homework to discuss as well as school plays, weekend arrangements, sports practices, game strategies and other preteen matters. They also, of course, use the phone to confide in one another and catch up on all the local gossip. Often they use the phone after supper for all of the above reasons because they're really quite busy during the day with school and extracurricular activities.

If you have more than one child in this age group and have your own telephone calls to make after work in the evening, a lot of conflicts can result. The question is, how do you democratically divide up the phone? Not only is there a time conflict to think about, but also phone calls cost money.

The first thing to ask yourself is whether or not you consider your ten-year-old child too young to have her own phone line. Since this is such an individual preference, I can't answer for every parent, but personally I don't think it's such a bad idea.

Deciding it's not an indulgence may solve your problem quite neatly. You will, of course, have to govern expenses and time use. I recommend, for example, that you not permit your child to make phone calls until all homework is completed or after bedtime. The phone may be unplugged overnight. If the phone rings during dinner, ask your child to say that she is eating now but that she will call the person back after dinner. Be prepared, however, for lots of excuses, such as, "Oh, I have to get the homework assignment from my friend." Be flexible. I think you'll know when and if the privilege is being abused.

Point out that telephones do cost money, and decide between you how much telephone use is sensible and permissible. Try to be reasonable about this. And I don't recommend charging the child for these calls. Because preteens aren't able to hold jobs, they really don't have access to much money.

If a separate phone line is out of the question, I suggest that, barring special situations, you set up a certain time period for phone socializing. Phone manners and phone etiquette should also be discussed. Messages can be taken and return calls made at an agreed-upon time.

As your family grows, more and more room must be made for each member that comes of age. It won't be long before your child will want to take "driver's education," and you know what will have to be shared then!

Fads

Your daughter wants to spray her hair green. She's eleven, and it seems like just yesterday that she was playing with dolls; but now she wants to imitate the older kids at school. She says that if you don't let her spray paint her hair, no one will like her. You tell her this is nonsense, and that she should stand up and be an individual and not go along with the crowd. But she answers, "I don't have any friends because you never let me do anything."

A child this age identifies with her peers and often with children slightly older than herself. These peers and older children become heroes and heroines in the younger child's eyes, and she wants to ape them in their gestures and in their dress. She feels that by doing this she, too, will become more mature and more sophisticated. Underneath the fads and the trappings is the normal desire to grow up.

The worst fear of the preteen is that she won't be accepted by her peers. A child voices this fear by saying that she has no friends. You know that the fear isn't logical, but you probably won't get anywhere trying to convince your child of this. The next time your child says to you, "I don't have any friends because you won't let me spray paint my hair," simply reply, "Well, if you want to look at it that way you can. If that's the only reason your friends want to be your friends—because you color your hair—hmmmm. . . ." Leave it at that. You don't have to be defensive, nor should you try to hammer in a message that she isn't ready to listen to.

Later when things are calmer around the house, invite your daughter to ask over one or two friends and suggest activities they might be interested in—baking something, listening to records together, doing homework together. Give her some constructive things to do with a friend. I can't guarantee that this will work, but perhaps your child just needs a nudge in the right direction.

Tell your daughter that everything has a time, and that you don't think it's the right time for her to go out in public with green hair. But you might suggest that she is ready for other sophisticated activities. Perhaps you can renegotiate her bedtime, or allow her to stay up to watch certain movies on television. Make sure she understands that she will be able to grow into these privileges, and that it's not as if she will never have them.

Be careful not to be too restrictive or arbitrary when it comes to fads. Although I don't think a child should go to school with green hair, there's no reason she can't have some fun with it at home on a weekend, as long as she agrees to wash it out before Monday morning. You might tell her that she can invite a friend in on Saturday night, when they can spray paint their hair and put on makeup as a harmless experiment. Very few fads in and of themselves are objectionable. They only become so in a certain context. Going to school dressed inappropriately demonstrates a lack of respect for the institution and the activities there. It might also, in some circumstances, suggest that your child belongs to a faster crowd than she really does. But flexibility is the key here. Try to negotiate an acceptable compromise with her.

A Fast Crowd

As your child grows older and spends more time away from you, it will be harder both to know whom she is associating with and what she is doing when she is in their company. When your child was small, you knew all her friends and could easily monitor her play and her associations. Now that she is older, this becomes a much more difficult task. And unfortunately, it's not going to get any easier as she moves into the teen years.

If you think your child is associating with a fast crowd, you have to evaluate what you mean by that. Perhaps you are comparing your child's friends with the kind of friends you had when you were her age, and they may seem fast when viewed against social mores of twenty years ago. Also, you may be basing your evaluation on hearsay or rumors. My first bit of advice is that you do some detective work and find out if these rumors have any basis in fact.

If you do find that your child is associating with children who are involved with drugs or alcohol or smoking, or who are flirting with danger by getting into older boys' cars, I think you have every right to try to limit the amount of time she spends with these people. During the preteen years, you do still have some control over whom your child sees and when. Much of this control will be lost as she matures into the teenage years.

Try to handle the matter delicately. If you are very harsh and rigidly restrictive, she may rebel, and then you'll really have a problem on your hands. The key is to be as diplomatic and as convincing as possible. Before you put your foot down and tell your child she can't ever see someone again, ask her to invite the person over for dinner so that you can begin to develop a little firsthand knowledge about her friends. It's possible that you may misjudge another child by her appearance. Perhaps an unkempt and wild-looking child will turn out to be a very sensitive person, someone you would actually like as a friend for your child.

If you do detect some attributes you don't like, engage your child in a conversation about the person, perhaps by saying, "I noticed that your friend seemed a bit sullen and moody." See what your child says. Gradually build a case that suggests that she might not benefit too much from her friend's value system. But do it cautiously. You don't want to get her back up so that she ends the conversation screaming, "But you never like my friends!"

If you perceive that your child is going off into a potentially dangerous situation, then I think you have the responsibility, regardless of the consequences, to try to protect her from that situation. Oddly enough, sometimes preteens will explore a risky situation, all the time hoping that their parents will set limits and prohibit them from going any further with the risk. Your job is to protect your child emotionally and physically from danger. She may fuss about it and may argue or even sneak around and keep company with a boy or a girl you disapprove of. It's very difficult to keep them from seeing each other totally; there are so many opportunities for them to get together when you're not around.

Don't be above impressing your child graphically by describing scenarios about what could happen to her if she continues to hang out with children who take drugs or who get into cars with older boys or strange men. Point out that sometimes the people who take girls into their cars are unstable, and that girls get robbed, molested and even killed.

If you are worried about your child and suspect that she is an excitement seeker, don't hesitate to hire someone during your absence to supervise her. I know of one working mother of a ten-year-old girl who has hired a young woman to be with her daughter after school to take her to various extracurricular activities and engage her in other enjoyable and stimulating events. The mother does this because she knows she has an adventurous child on her hands who without supervision would be tempted to get into trouble. The girl hates the supervision, by the way, but you shouldn't let the child's dislike of the situation sway your decision making if you feel the child is at risk.

You can also involve yourself positively in your child's dilemma by providing her with weekend activities under your supervision, and suggesting she ask a friend along—a friend that you approve of and like. An inviting home environment, family outings and an accepting attitude are important.

Try your very best to be empathic; see things through her eyes. It is essential that you maintain a close relationship in which you can talk openly to each other. She will need a lot of protection and guidance as she moves further into the throes of puberty.

Preteen Dating

There is no absolutely "correct" age for children to start dating, although the average in this country is between fifteen and sixteen years. That doesn't mean to say that you should forbid, before that age, any kind of social excursion with the opposite sex. Rather, treat such episodes as unique events and use them to begin formulating guidelines for the future.

At this age, children associate with the opposite sex more than they did during the earlier school years—usually in social groups, but occasionally good friendships (and sometimes even romantic involvements) develop between preteens of the opposite sex. Because your child may find herself in these relationships, she will need practice in socializing with boys. This practice should be gradual, however, experienced in small increments over a long period so that when she is old enough to date, she will have had time to master the necessary social skills.

A good way to begin the dating experience is with daytime group activities such as sporting events, skating parties and beach parties, followed by double-dating. Double-dating can be viewed as an intermediate step, with single dating reserved as something your child can look forward to as she grows and demonstrates increasingly good judgment. Double-dating may have the effect of postponing intimate entanglements, and, because another friend is along, may make your child feel more comfortable.

A double date, however, does not insure safety. Preteens don't yet have flawless judgment—nor are they immune to peer pressure. Some parents, in fact, have told me that they sometimes prefer their preteens to be in the company of only one or two other children their age because group activities can sometimes get out of hand. Some children seem to be extremely impressionable and unable to think for themselves in group situations. Others may tend to show off or to be defiant. Parents must also consider the potential for drug and alcohol use, sexual intimacy or dangerous automobile travel in any group activity they are thinking of letting their children participate in.

Talk to your child about the whole issue of dating. Guidelines and rules are helpful because they provide a structure for her to rely on in new and uncomfortable situations. If you have told your daughter that it's dangerous to ride in an automobile with someone who is drinking, she may be able to rely on that statement when trying to counteract peer pressure. Children also internalize many of the values you impart. It won't do much good to keep them to yourself, so share them with your child.

You can also get involved in another helpful way. You might offer advice about what to wear, where to go, how to get there and who should pay. Perhaps your child might like the idea of a Dutch treat, since this would allow her to feel equal in a relationship with a boy. Perhaps she might also like some suggestions as to how to say "no," should an unpleasant situation arise.

As the parent of a preteen, you are responsible for protecting her— and this protection extends to her social life as well as her physical life. Monitor your child's activities. Find out exactly where she will be going, with whom, what they will be doing, whether or not there will be other adults present, and what means of transportation will be used. If you are unclear about the nature of the activity, contact one of the other parents with your questions, and if necessary coordinate supervision and pickup times.

Showing an interest in your child's social life will demonstrate that you care about her well-being. When you have satisfied yourself that all is well, wish her a good time. When she comes home, again show an interest, but don't give her the third degree. Keep in mind that this social activity is an opportunity for her to develop relationships that are independent of the family, and that she will need to have some measure of privacy in which to do this.

Sex

Sex is a very delicate matter with a preteen. On the one hand, you don't want to be intrusive, yet on the other, you don't want to be laissez-faire about the issue either.

As the parent of a preteen, you are responsible for guiding your child in matters of sexual involvement, much as you have been guiding her in other areas. It's to be hoped that you have given her a good education in sexual matters, both so that she has a clear understanding of what sex is all about, and also that you and she will have a history of talking about sex together. The conversations you have with your child about the extent of her romantic relationships should be an extension of her sex education.

Before you begin talking to your child about sexual activities, however, make sure you are clear in your own mind what exactly you mean by "having sex." There are many gradations of experience. There's minimal physical contact such as hand-holding, hugging and putting an arm around someone's shoulder. There's rubbing up against someone when dancing. And there's an array of kissing, fondling and petting activities. These activities may go on for years without necessarily leading to sexual intercourse. Be clear in your own mind where you would draw the line for your child. This doesn't mean that you will actually be able to draw the line, but it will help you both if you yourself are clear about where that line is when you first talk to your child.

Many parents shy away from thinking about specifics when it comes to their children's sexuality. They do this either out of embarrassment or out of a misplaced notion of prurience. But it's a mistake to leave yourself in a confused, vague state when discussing this issue with your child. Sex is not an easy topic for anybody to talk over, but I do think it is important to organize your own thoughts before you discuss them with your child.

Don't take the sexual issue out of the context of the rest of a relationship. Before you can discuss the difficult matter of sex, take an interest in other aspects of your child's relationship with a person of the opposite sex. Try to keep abreast of their activities. Determine whether the other child is considerate or not. Learn where they go together and what they do. Find out what their interests are and who their friends are. If they have a spat, watch how it is handled. Your child may need some help in this area, too. If you just pull sexuality out of context, you will find it much more difficult to deal with. If you are involved more generally in your child's affairs, however, you can be a better guide.

But don't try to get too involved. That's not fair to her. She is, after all, trying to develop an independent relationship with someone outside the family. This is a normal thing to do.

Once you have done all your homework, then you can begin a series of *conversations* on sexual matters. Notice that I have made that plural. One conversation at one sitting will accomplish very little; rather, you should have a running conversation over a long period of time, as you would in other interpersonal relationships.

You might introduce the matter by saying to your child that often there is a romantic aspect to a relationship, and ask her how that is going. "Romantic" is usually understood, even by preteens, as a euphemism for sexual. She may blush and be evasive, but don't let the matter just drop. Indicate that you are available to talk to her about any questions she may have about this important issue. Perhaps you could tell her that when you were her age, you had lots of questions, too, and you were lucky enough to have the kind of parent you could discuss them with. Or perhaps, if the reverse was true, you could say that you weren't so lucky, but that you would certainly like to make yourself available to her if there are any questions.

As the conversations progress, begin to talk in specifics. Now that you are clear in your own mind what activities you think are acceptable for a child her age to engage in—and I *don't* think an eleven- or twelve-year-old should be engaging in sexual intercourse—do not hesitate to tell her your thoughts. Most important, be sure to tell her that you hope she will never engage in any activities in which she doesn't feel entirely comfortable. Let her know that you can help her with strategies to avoid such situations.

Be alert to the fact that your child might be looking to you to help her set limits. A twelve-year-old is a bit young to be dating steadily, and it is possible that she may be feeling pressure to sleep with a boy or engage in some sexual activity that she's not yet ready for. Let her know that her own sexual desires are normal. But remind her of the implications of a sexual relationship. Be truthful about your attitudes and opinions and allow her to reveal her point of view. You may, by defining clear limits of what you think is acceptable and what is not, be able to help her out. Indeed, she may actually feel quite relieved.

You should monitor your child's activities and try to let her know that you can be counted on for support. Avoid the trap of simply nagging and lecturing to her. Although you may be experiencing a good deal of anxiety yourself, try to be empathic.

Guiding a child through the complex issue of sexual relationships with others is one aspect of preteen sexuality. Another is sexual curiosity:

> My son is ten years old. Today I had to do a major cleaning in his room, and I turned his mattress over. Underneath it, I found a collection of "girlie" magazines. I was really taken aback and a little upset. I had no idea that sex had even occurred to him. I don't know whether to put them back and forget about it, or confront him about it.

There are several issues here. First, the mother was in her son's room and going through his things. Second is that her son had hidden the magazines. Then there is the issue of his sexual curiosity and her surprise at discovering this. Last is the potentially exploitative nature of some of these kinds of magazines. Let's look at the issues separately.

Some people have the attitude that if they find something, the other person really meant for them to find it. I don't think that's the case here. If an object is hidden under one thing and then under something else, it probably wasn't meant to be found. The next question is, should the mother admit that she was in her son's room cleaning up and that she found the magazines? My opinion is that she should. Unless she was actually snooping, which I would consider invasive, she should simply tell her son the truth. She was giving his room a good going-over and happened to stumble upon these magazines.

A child's interest in sex is perfectly natural at this age. Therefore a parent needn't be embarrassed at finding the magazines, nor should she shame or humiliate the child. Sex is certainly a healthy matter to be curious about, and at the preteen age, he probably hasn't had a lot of opportunity to look at nude women. So have a light touch when you talk to your own youngster if you find yourself in this situation. Say you understand why he might want to look at such magazines, and that it's perfectly natural that he might find them exciting.

But...

Actually there are two "buts." The first is similar to the situation in which you find your preschooler "playing doctor" with a playmate. Although you cannot stop your son from looking at magazines, and although this interest is fundamentally healthy, you, in your role as a socializer, should not be in the position of promoting such activities. Tell your son that you would rather he not bring these magazines home. Besides, you might add, it's against the law for him to purchase them because he is underage, another reason that you really cannot condone his owning them.

I also think you might want to take this opportunity to point out to him the exploitative nature of some of these magazines. Make it clear that his gradual development into a sexual person should include more than simple anatomical and mechanical involvement. Talk about affection and feelings and caring for another person—not just exploiting another or being opportunistic for his own desires. Try not to be preachy, but make him aware that such magazines lean in the direction of using women merely as stimulants for sexual interest, and that while there is nothing wrong with sexual curiosity or excitement per se, such images can present a distorted picture of reality by omitting many other aspects of sex within an affectionate relationship.

Don't make too big a deal about the magazines, though, because you risk being thought of as a prude. That is not the worst thing in the world, except that you want your son to be able to talk over sexual matters with you and your spouse if he feels the need to. At his age, these magazines are probably not habitual reading material anyway.

Another preteen sexual issue is masturbation. Many parents become concerned that their children masturbate and wonder whether they should talk to them about it or not. My answer to this question is quite simple: Mind your own business. Preteens do masturbate before puberty, and it's perfectly normal in the developing child. When your son reaches puberty, you may even find evidence of nocturnal emissions — ejaculations during sleep. Some abstract mention about nocturnal emissions during a "birds and bees" discussion is enough to let him know it is healthy and common. It's not necessary or even desirable to draw a child's attention to the fact that you know that he masturbates. Be aware of it, discuss it with your spouse, and know that it's a normal function. But let your child have his privacy.

Drugs, Cigarettes and Alcohol

While the individual consequences of smoking, drinking and taking drugs are quite different, the three issues are similar in that they represent inappropriate activities for any child, and they all pose serious emotional, physical and social hazards.

Let me make it clear that I do not condone the smoking of cigarettes, the taking of drugs or the drinking of alcohol for children under any circumstances. But let me also make it clear that you cannot just forbid these activities and hope to make an impression on your child. Educating your child about restraint in the face of peer pressure, about the damage that such bad habits can do and about the legal and physical consequences of using these substances will take a great deal of time, patience and restraint on your part. It is not an easy job, but it is an absolutely vital one.

Begin by helping your child become aware of the problems involved in drinking, smoking and drug taking. You can call attention to them in several ways.

In urban environments or even in suburban centers, many times we are with our children when we see people who are inebriated or who are obviously high on drugs — or worse, who are suffering the consequences of having taken too much alcohol or drugs. Usually we just rush by, either oblivious to the scene ourselves or not wanting to make our children aware that such situations exist. I think, however, that these occasions, as unpleasant as they are to focus on and think about, are excellent learning experiences for children. If you are on an errand with your daughter and notice such a person, stand a safe distance away, but do not neglect to point out the person to your child. "Isn't that awful!" you might begin. "Do you know what is the matter with that boy? Although he looks sick, he's not sick in the sense that he has the flu. He's feeling sick because he took drugs. What do you think about somebody who would do that to himself?"

When you are watching the news on TV or reading the newspaper and you come across a story about a drunk-driving accident or a crackdown on drugs, point out the article or news story to your child. "You know, they're growing crops that are used not for food, but for people to take as drugs. People will steal and kill and make themselves sick using those drugs." Although drugs and alcohol may not yet be a part of your child's immediate reality, you will be helping him organize his thoughts about the matter in a kindly, conversational way—making him aware of the dangers, but not coming down too hard on him personally.

You can also help your child to turn away from drugs, alcohol and cigarettes by being a model for restraint yourself. I'm not suggesting by this that you should become a teetotaler, or that parents don't have rights that children don't have, but do keep in mind that if you smoke in front of your child, you are on shaky ground when you try to prohibit your child from smoking. This same principle holds true for alcohol. If you habitually drink beer, wine or hard liquor but tell your child that this is a bad habit and that he may not touch alcohol, it is impossible for your child not to intuit the hypocrisy in your message. While you certainly are within your own rights to drink if you want to, remember that your *practical* task of teaching your preteen not to drink will probably be more difficult than that of the parent who doesn't drink or who drinks only occasionally.

If you do not have the habit yourself, you can serve as a model for your child. Let's say that you do not smoke. It will then be easier for you to talk to your child about smoking. "The reason I don't smoke is that it damages the lungs, it's bad for my skin, it causes heart palpitations and heart disease and a host of different cancers. Certainly if you want to be a dancer or a sprinter, you won't succeed if you smoke." When you and your child enter a restaurant, you can make a point of asking the waiter if there is a no-smoking section. If you are out with your child and happen to see someone who is sick and coughing from cigarette smoke, you can point this out and perhaps mention someone you know who smoked for many years and now has emphysema. With these conversations, it's to be hoped that your child will absorb some of what you are saying. When the temptation comes up for him to smoke, he may perhaps experiment with it, but may eventually find a way to excuse himself from the activity. If you yourself smoke, however, you obviously can't be a model for healthy behavior.

Or let's say that you do not drink habitually or take drugs. You can then say to your child: "I value my mind. I depend on my mind to carry me through life. Alcohol and drugs interfere with how my mind functions. I've invested too much in getting my head to work right to mess it up with drugs or alcohol."

This doesn't mean that you should be excessively moralistic and rigid about forbidding alcohol. Nor do I think that you, as an adult, should abstain if the occasion—whether festive, religious or social—arises. Preteens are not so immature that they cannot tell the difference between this kind of behavior and the kind that gets people into trouble.

On the other hand, I don't think it's necessary to offer your ten-year-old a glass of wine or champagne on social occasions. Some parents feel that if they introduce their children to alcohol gradually in the home environment, the children will learn to use alcohol in moderation. I'm not sure that's such a good idea. First of all, alcohol is not healthy for the growing child. Second, introducing alcohol to a child suggests that you condone drinking—even to the point where you want to teach your child how to drink. A sip for the curious child is one thing; serving him a welcoming, encouraging drink of his own is quite another.

Children will experiment, despite all your prudent measures. You may even catch your child in the act and have a confrontation about the issue. A parent once came to me and said that she had found a pack of cigarettes in her daughter's jacket and didn't know what to do. The mother was tired of nagging her daughter to put her jacket away and had taken it off the back of the chair to put it away herself. She noticed a bulge, and when she looked into the pocket, she found the cigarettes. She didn't know whether or not to tell her daughter she had found them, worried that her daughter might retort, "What were you doing in my jacket?" But because she herself didn't smoke, and because she knew how sick cigarette smoking could make a person, she decided to confront her daughter. "I found a pack of cigarettes in your jacket," she said.

The daughter quickly answered: "Oh, they're not mine. I'm just holding them for a friend."

Fortunately, the mother had her wits about her and, to her credit, answered: "Well, if you are a good friend to this girl, I don't think you should hold cigarettes for her. You should tell her the dangers of ciga-rette smoking, and that since she is your friend you want her to be in good shape and to stay healthy."

The daughter, wanting to end the conversation, nodded, and even went so far as to add the next day that she had told her friend all about the dangers of smoking and that she would not hold the cigarettes for her anymore. But two days later, a neighbor called the mother and reported that she had seen her daughter walking along the street with a group of girls, and that the daughter was smoking.

When the daughter came home from school, her mother told her what she had heard. The daughter burst into tears. "Don't you trust me?" she wailed. "I told you I didn't smoke."

The evidence was quite clear, but the mother knew she was not going to get a confession. Instead she used it as an occasion to further educate her daughter about smoking. "Look," she said, "we don't want you to smoke. Obviously you can sneak it, and once in a while you are going to get caught. But it's an awful habit. There are people who are dying because of it. There are people who wish they had never smoked be-cause now they can't stop. Maybe you think it's cool. Maybe you think you look sophisticated and grown-up. Perhaps it makes you feel comfort-able in social situations, and you are practicing to be a grown-up. But I am here to tell you that there are other ways to practice being a grown-up besides sticking a cigarette in your mouth and smoking it, and we would hope that you not only would not smoke, but that you would not lie to us about it."

Talking to your child about drugs, alcohol and smoking is a difficult matter. On the one hand, you have every right to try to impress dramati-cally upon him the dangers of these substances. On the other, you don't want to bludgeon him into blind obedience through very strict punish-ments, because then the child will never learn to think for himself. And once you are absent from his daily life—or not present at any given moment—he will not be able to stand up for himself and have opinions of his own. You have to help him develop good judgment so that when someone taunts him or tempts him, he will have the wherewithal to turn away.

You can also help your child turn down alcohol, drugs or cigarettes by providing him with excuses. Say to your preteen, "Listen, a lot of kids around you are probably going to start smoking cigarettes; other kids are going to tell you that you should start smoking joints; and some might start taking other drugs or drinking. I know that at times it will be very hard to turn these things down. You might be afraid that the other kids will think you're a baby. They may try very hard to talk you into it. I want to give you some excuses that you can use to beg the issue. You could say to them that you're allergic and that it makes you sick. You could say you've tried it before and that it doesn't do much for you. You can say it gives you a headache or that your skin breaks out, or that you're on some medication that's incompatible with whatever they are offering you."

Although I'm not in favor of teaching your child to lie, I do think there are times when children need "protective" lies so that they will not suffer harshly from their own good decisions, and so that they will not succumb to the kind of intense peer pressure that can surround the issue of drugs, alcohol and cigarettes.

It seems to me that when parents are temperate and avoid extreme and harsh reactions, their children will have an easier time handling these tough and potentially dangerous matters.

Cheating, Lying and Stealing

Strictly speaking, prior to the school-age years, a child cannot be said to be cheating, lying or stealing. As I discussed in a previous section, because a preschooler's sense of logic is not fully developed, and because that preschooler can sometimes still inhabit a world in which wishes take precedence over reality, he cannot always reliably tell right from wrong. By the time he has entered elementary school, however, and certainly by the time he has reached the preteen years, his moral judgment should be well developed. Thus, the issues of cheating, lying and stealing have to be dealt with in a more serious manner.

Cheating, lying and stealing should not be tolerated in any child who has reached the preteen years—although as we will see in a moment, some kinds of lies may be exceptions to the rule. You should make every effort to help your child with these complex moral and ethical issues.

First, let's look at cheating. It's common to see a child cheat when playing games at school or when doing schoolwork or homework. A child may argue with an umpire that a certain shot was in or out— knowing full well that the reverse was true—in order to win the game. Other children may copy answers from classmates—either with their cooperation, or on the sly.

Although virtually all preteens know the difference between right and wrong, that doesn't necessarily mean that all will have the feelings that go along with knowing that difference. Some children who are fully aware that an action or utterance is deceitful, but care only that they not get caught, may have a conscience that functions improperly or erratically. Preteens are not the only ones with faulty consciences; given enough temptation and only a slim probability of detection, many adults will cheat or lie or steal. It's a fact of human nature, and shows only how powerful the urge to bend the rules is. Guiding your preteen through these temptations is of utmost importance.

Let's say you've received a call from the school telling you that your son has been caught cheating on a test. First, ask yourself *why* your preteen is cheating. There are several reasons a ten- or eleven-year-old might cheat. Perhaps the child simply does not know the work. In this sense, cheating is like stealing. He is taking something away from someone else because he does not have it himself. Of course, we know that the boy is also stealing from himself, because he is not learning the skills he needs.

As the parent of such a child, do a little investigating. Is the material at school too hard for your son? Did he get too far behind because of illness? Is the child able to find the time to study—or do sports, friends and watching television get in the way? Does your child have poor study habits?

Or is the problem that he has developed the attitude that he doesn't have to work for anything? Does he believe that he can fake his way through life?

If the issue is cheating at games, perhaps the central conflict is power or status. Sometimes a child who is competing at a game thinks that if he can get around a rule or out-argue the other side or the referee, he will be more acceptable to his circle of friends.

Once you have ferreted out the possible reasons for the cheating, then you have to deal with the matter at hand. Make it clear at once that cheating is unacceptable—*no matter what the reason*. Even if it's because your child did not know the work and is cheating to catch up with the rest of the class, make sure he understands that this is wrong. You will have to offer him extra help or get him moved to a class that is more in line with his abilities—but it's important to demonstrate that you feel sincerely and profoundly upset by the fact that he has cheated, and that you view it as a serious problem.

Many parents inadvertently teach their children to cheat by enjoying a clever deceit themselves—whether the fraud is as simple as accepting the wrong change from the grocer and being tickled about it or cheating on your income taxes and bragging about how you got away with it. Although I do not mean to imply that all children who are cheats become so because their parents are, I do think you have to look at your own life and your own values. Make sure that you do all you can to instill honorable values in your child, and demonstrate that cheating is not a desirable goal—nor is it a positive achievement in any way.

You should be quite stern when you first learn that your child is cheating, but unless you discover the root of the problem, I doubt that punishment alone will do much good. Many times a very serious discussion and the demonstration of your extreme displeasure, combined with his having been caught, will stop a novice cheater cold. Many younger children do not pay much attention to the morality of the issue and may one time copy someone else's homework and not give it another thought. If you catch your child at it, however, you have an excellent opportunity to stop this behavior early. Cheating often begins in a very benign way, without much malice, but once a child learns that he can get away with it, it may become a deeply ingrained habit that is considerably more difficult to break.

Lying is a very complicated issue, one that philosophers have struggled with for centuries. There are so many kinds of lying, so many shades of gray. There is lying to cover up an offense. There is lying to enhance one's status—exaggeration. There is the white lie used to avoid hurting someone else's feelings. And there is lying out of fear of severe retribution for some action. Some children lie only occasionally; others become habitual liars. Dealing with a lie your child tells is a very difficult matter. It is not as clear-cut as helping a child with toilet training or with bedtime rituals. Because teaching a child to be honest involves the training of a mental attitude and is at the heart of both private and public ethics and morality, the issue doesn't lend itself to inflexible rules and regulations.

It is not beyond the ability of a preteen to tell the difference among the various kinds of lies. Parents can tell the difference; and by the age of ten or eleven, so can children. The most intelligent course of action a parent can take to help a child with the issue of lying is to talk about moral choices and about the different kinds of lies.

Many lies fall into the category of the cover-up. Let's say a child steals five dollars from your wallet. You confront him because you suspect that he has taken the money, and out of a desire not to get caught, or to cover up the crime, he lies to you. "Who, me? No way," he says. As the parent, you have a real dilemma. If you strongly suspect or even know that your child has taken the money and is lying, I think you should tell him so. A strongly suspected lie should not go without comment. The child may then vehemently defend his lie, but it is important to point out to him that you suspect the lie has taken place. It is possible that you are mistaken—and if you are and discover it, then by all means apologize to the child. If you make a mistake but don't discover it, it is still better to impress upon a child how very much you abhor a lie and how very wrong a cover-up is than to let the lie slide because you aren't 100 percent positive it really is one. But please do not be quick to accuse and to judge.

Even if you are positive, however, and even if your preteen admits that he did tell a lie, you still have an interesting dilemma. Do you punish your child for stealing the money, or do you reward him for confessing the truth? If you punish the child harshly for the theft, you may encourage him to lie at a later date. On the other hand, stealing itself is a serious offense, and you cannot let that go either. My advice is to have a long talk with your child. Tell him that you are very pleased that he told you the truth—that, in the long run, his ability to tell you the truth is central to the whole issue of his morality. But make it clear that you are very upset about his having stolen the money, and that should it ever happen again, certain privileges will be taken away from him. Perhaps you could engage your son in a discussion of the appropriate consequences for this offense. In addition to any other steps you take, he should return the money to you.

In general, you will have less difficulty with your child's lying if you are able to reduce the incentives for it. A child who fears excessive retaliation for even minor offenses will learn very early on that to lie is to protect himself. No child is perfect, and even the best of preteens will occasionally do something inadvisable. If your child intuits that you will react very punitively to his wrongdoing, he may be tempted to lie and may become, as time goes on, a habitual liar.

Another kind of lie that cannot go unnoticed—because it, too, can become a very unfortunate habit—is the self-aggrandizing lie, or the exaggeration. "My Dad is president of the company" or "I made five hundred dollars this summer" or "I saw Bruce Springsteen in person in the city yesterday" are examples of untruths uttered in order to enhance one's status with one's peers. If you hear your own preteen exaggerate, gently point out, without shaming the child, that what he has said is not strictly accurate, and that he should try to be as truthful as possible, since his credibility with others will be damaged if he isn't.

I'm not convinced that any additional punishments are necessary for the self-aggrandizing lie. If the exaggerations are not habitual and are mild, simply pointing out that *you* know he knows what he said isn't true may stop the behavior. After all, it's embarrassing to be caught in that kind of a lie, and just the exposure itself may put an end to it. If, however, you notice that your preteen is constantly exaggerating, try to investigate the reasons for his false self-enhancement. Does your son lack confidence in himself? Why does he feel he needs to resort to this kind of lie to impress his friends? If the problem seems severe, I suggest a consultation with a psychologist.

Another kind of lie is one that even adults struggle with: the white lie. You may find that from time to time you even encourage your preteen to lie, if you feel that the truth will hurt someone else or himself unnecessarily. "Don't tell Grandma that you hate her present this Christmas. Try to act as if you really like it, because she spent four months making it for you." "Don't tell Dad we were at the record store today. I want to surprise him for his birthday." "Why don't you tell Eileen that you have a cold if you don't want to go to her party?" "If someone offers you a drink, just simply say that alcohol makes you vomit."

Most preteens are mature enough to understand the differences among the cover-up lie, the exaggeration and the white lie. They also are mature enough to have developed empathy, and will understand that the white lie is often necessary in the service of not hurting other people's feelings. But to be sure that your child knows, discuss the matter with him—not once, but often. The realm of ethics and morality is complex and abstract and cannot be absorbed by any preteen on only one occasion.

A preteen's best teacher and model is you. When confronted with a moral choice, allow your preteen to be privy to the matter and discuss the various possibilities aloud in front of him. Perhaps on occasion you could even ask his advice. In this way, your child will become accustomed to coping with the complexities of morality, and will have a caring and mature guide to help him.

*   *   *

Stealing involves fraud and deceit, much as lying and cheating do—but stealing is a more clear-cut issue for parents to deal with.

There are many reasons why children steal. Very young children without a well-developed sense of personal property may experiment with stealing small items from shops or candy from grocery stores. Other children lack self-discipline or any notion of restraint and steal out of an immediate desire for self-gratification. Others steal to increase their status with their peers. Either the act itself is seen as daring, or the items acquired during the theft are valued by the group. Still other children steal as a message that all is not going well in other areas of their development. Children who steal are likely to be noncompliant and to have a variety of problems.

Stealing is a very serious issue. It is one of the most pervasive forms of misbehavior among preteens, and is now thought to be much more prevalent among children this age than was previously imagined.

How a parent deals with stealing will depend on the age of the child and the motivation behind the theft. If your child is on the youngish side and you have reason to suspect that this is a first offense, explain to him that what he has taken does not belong to him, and that it is someone else's property. Just the embarrassment of getting caught will make most young children stop stealing. You should also march your child back to the store from which he took the item, have him apologize to the salesclerk and have him make restitution. If the item has not been consumed or damaged, the child should give it back. Otherwise he should pay for the item either out of his allowance or by working off the cost at home at some extremely boring chore.

Under no circumstances should stealing go without exposure or without a confrontation. Small children who experiment and then learn that they can get away with stealing may be tempted to steal yet again. Preteens who are not found out or not made to suffer the consequences of theft may begin to believe that your complacency means complicity, and that you are tolerant of this behavior. Although confronting your preteen may be unpleasant and difficult, it is absolutely vital that you do so.

Sometimes your child will lie to you about an item that you suspect he has stolen. Be wary of accepting explanations, no matter how clever. If you really think the item was stolen, you should say so. Ask your son a long series of questions to pin him down and to cause him a bit of heat. Making him anxious may stop the behavior.

Simply admonishing a child for the theft—or even punishing him by exposure and by making him perform very dull chores—will not be enough. It is also essential that you find out the reasons for the child's stealing behavior. If your child lacks restraint and self-discipline, then you and he will have to work on these problems in the immediate future. If the reason is self-aggrandizement, try to find out why your son feels so inadequate that he has to resort to stealing to be accepted by his peers. If your child is involved with a group of friends who get their kicks by stealing, then do not hesitate to remove him from this group. Be aware that your son may be the ringleader; it's a good idea to break up such a gang.

Vandalism

There are many possible reasons why a preteen might engage in vandalism. Some children participate in wanton destruction, like breaking windows at school, merely because they think it's fun and get carried away on the spur of the moment. For some, damaging property is a form of antisocial behavior and may be a means of expressing resentment and anger. Perhaps your child is very upset and unhappy with you and is taking out his anger by defacing property. Or perhaps the anger is more specifically directed at the place where the damage occurs: If a child breaks school windows, he may be furious with the school or someone in the school.

Other children participate in vandalism to see how much they can get away with. They might break into a school building and take a piece of equipment, not because they want or need it, but because it represents a perverse challenge. Some engage in destruction of property because such behavior is a rebellious testing of the limits. Still others seek risk and excitement. Some preteens, in fact, seek excitement to ward off depression. This is more common in children who are a bit older, but it does sometimes occur in the preteen years. And finally, some children may engage in vandalism as a way of expressing their individuality.

Vandalism should not be taken lightly. You have to deal with the matter in two ways: first, by finding out the reason for the vandalism and treating that; and second, by exposing the child and making him face the consequences of his action.

If there are troubles in the home that seem to be triggering the vandalism, then these problems will have to be attended to. If your child is engaging in vandalism out of a need to express his uniqueness, you will have to help him find other ways. If your child is an excitement seeker, try to learn what it is he feels is lacking in his life. If your child is depressed, he may need professional help to cope with his depression in a more appropriate manner.

Finding out the underlying reason doesn't mean, however, that you should gloss over the act of vandalism itself. Of course, you must check the facts and be sure that the allegation is true. It is absolutely vital that you deal with the issue at once and express a proper amount of moral outrage. You will be met with a host of flimsy excuses: "Oh, we were just kidding around"; "It doesn't hurt anybody"; "It's just the school, and it won't cost anybody anything"; but make it clear that such excuses don't impress you, and point out the fallacy in them. Even if it's the first time the child has engaged in vandalism—in fact, *especially* if it's the first time—you should express your disappointment, bring the child to the scene of the crime, have the child confess that he did it, and have him make plans for restitution. If his friends were also involved, he should not have to shoulder the entire responsibility.

I don't think it's necessary to punish the child further than that. The humiliation of being exposed, the cost in time or money for the restoration, as well as the disappointment and outrage you express should solve the problem. You will, of course, have to try to find out what prompted the vandalism, and you should try to remove your son from the company of the group who did it. Although it's always easier to think that your son was influenced by others, keep in mind that he may have been an instigator. Repeated antisocial acts should be attended to by a mental-health professional in addition to the steps I have outlined. The important thing is to take swift action and be clear and direct. Do not trivialize or treat such actions as harmless pranks.

SPECIAL CONSIDERATIONS

Not all discipline considerations fit neatly into chronological categories. Several unique contemporary topics cut across all age levels—the question of what to tell a caregiver about disciplining your child; how to share the discipline of your child in a joint custody situation; how to handle discipline if you are a single parent; how to manage your child if you are disabled; how discipline decisions may differ from the norm if you have an exceptional child; and how to cope with discipline if you are a stepparent or if one is present in your household. These are difficult and complex concerns. Each topic could easily fill a separate volume, but I want to at least call attention to these special circumstances and outline some of the central issues involved.

CAREGIVERS

A great deal of thought and preparation is needed when introducing a caregiver into your child's life. Both the child and the caregiver will have to be prepared. A gradual introductory period will limit the degree of adjustment and stress for both your child and the caregiver. That, of course, will in turn lower the probability of discipline problems. The smoother the transition, the more comfortable everyone will feel and the less likely there will be stress.

If it is at all possible, the caregiver should visit the home several times prior to her employment. When she comes, she should not participate directly in the child care, but merely observe. These visits will serve three purposes. First, the caregiver will be able to see how you care for your child and then model herself after your style. Second, by coming to your home on several occasions, she will become a familiar person to the child. And third, these visits will give you a chance to watch her reactions to the way you deal with your child. Does she seem critical? Do you sense that she would discipline your child more punitively than you do? If that seems the case, now is the time to find out—not six months after you have hired her.

In selecting and training a caregiver, make sure that you hire someone with views about discipline similar to your own. To do this, you will have to make sure that she clearly understands your philosophy of discipline, and that she is flexible enough to adjust her style to yours if need be. After the caregiver has visited you and watched you in action, ask her to tell you what she would do in a similar situation. Keep in mind that the caregiver will be the one implementing the discipline. For those hours during which she is in charge of your child, she will be responsible. Therefore, explain to her your philosophy in as much detail as you can so that there will be no surprises. And make sure that you build into your schedule and hers enough time at the end of the day to discuss what happened during the day and how various situations were handled. Telling the caregiver your philosophy of discipline also has the added benefit of forcing you to organize your own thoughts about the subject.

If your children are old enough, you can let them get involved in the selection process. After an older child has met the caregiver, ask him what he thinks of the person and to offer any suggestions he might have. (That doesn't mean you have to agree!)

After hiring a caregiver, you may discover that your child reacts very badly to her. The parents of twins told me that they had hired a house-keeper, and that the children were just horrible to her—running out into the street when she took them for walks, deliberately spilling their milk onto the floor, disobeying her every chance they got. It was, said the parents, not unlike the way a classroomful of students will some-times behave if left with a substitute teacher. The reasons for the twins' behavior was pretty clear. They were angry with their parents for leaving them with a surrogate caregiver, and were hoping by their bad behavior to either get her fired or get her to quit. The parents, however, thought the caregiver was doing a good job and decided to sit down with the two children and have a little talk. "Listen, we like her," the parents said. "We think she is really good. No matter what you do, no matter how much you carry on, we're not going to fire her. It's not your decision." The talk turned out to be very beneficial to all concerned. As soon as the children realized their tactics weren't going to get rid of the caregiver, they stopped terrorizing her.

Once you have settled on the person you want to care for your child, be very clear about what you want her to do in your absence. Try to spell out in great detail the routines at home, the ones your child is most comfortable with. If your child is used to a story before lunch, tell the caregiver that. Not having that piece of information, the caregiver may unwittingly omit the story or try to tell it after lunch, thus provoking an unnecessary conflict.

Discuss possible infractions and provide examples of what you want done. Also be sure to include what you do not want said or done. Be explicit. "Don't call her a 'bad girl,' please"; "We do not approve of scaring her with threats of punishment or horror tales"; or "I'd prefer not having comparisons made in order to get her to obey." You should spell out in detail what you consider appropriate discipline for your child as well as which issues you do not want to end in conflict. "If she doesn't finish her milk, that's okay."

If you expect the caregiver to do household chores, then you should plan how the child is going to be taken care of during that time. This is an area for potential disaster. The caregiver, rushing to accomplish all the chores before you get home, may shortchange your child and treat her more harshly than she deserves, because all the while she is think-ing: "I have to get this done before your mother gets home." Make your priorities clear.

JOINT CUSTODY

When a child lives in two different households, there will almost certainly be differences in routines, differences in expectations of the child and differences in personalities. But uniformity in child rearing can't be expected, even in a single household. If the approaches of the two parents are too disparate, however, it will cause a great deal of strain on the child. Having to switch back and forth, back and forth, between very different kinds of discipline can produce stress and anxiety for the child.

Children are paradoxical. On the one hand, they can adapt fairly well to a normal amount of disparity. The best analogy I can think of is the child in the home of bilingual parents. Quickly learning which parent speaks what language, the child will unconsciously address the parent in the correct language, and will usually learn to speak both languages fluently without tremendous effort or emotional strain.

To some extent a child who is the product of a joint custody arrangement may also learn to speak both "languages" of discipline—unless, as I have just said, the approaches are too different. So in that sense, children *can* adapt. But the other side of the paradox is that children may either show the strain of the switch-over, or they may try to use the situation to their advantage. It is not uncommon to have a child come home to you after having spent time with the other parent and complain that "things weren't done that way *there.*"

To minimize any problems that can develop, it is very important for you and your ex-spouse to maintain some level of decorum and civility so that you can discuss on a regular basis events that have come up in each of your homes. Work out mutually agreeable ways to manage these situations with your child. Although complete consistency is not possible, or even ideal, some level of compatibility in your discipline styles is vital for your child.

Be alert to the fact that when there is a divorce, other motives sometimes lurk behind differences of opinion about discipline. Some parents who are either eager to win their child over or who feel guilty about the divorce may lean too much toward indulgence. Then, decisions about discipline are not made in the child's best interest, but because the parent has his or her own interest in mind.

Also be wary of handling your child too punitively simply because he reminds you too much of your ex-spouse. Parents sometimes confess that they become enraged at their children because they look, talk or act like an ex-spouse. An adult has to remind herself that she is blaming the child for having some attributes of the despised ex-mate.

Any couple contemplating separation should make plans to have regular discussions about their child's rearing, including discipline issues, even if there are no apparent differences in philosophy or specific problems. (Even parents who aren't having marital problems should do this.)

Because some disagreements between ex-spouses are inevitable, tell your child that you recognize that there are and will be differences. Acknowledge how difficult it can be for the child by saying, "I know how annoying it is when I expect you to do x, y and z in this house, when in Mom's house, you don't have to." If there are problems, tell the child that you will take the issue up with your ex-mate and that you will try to minimize the differences. But do remind him that a certain amount of disagreement will exist, that this is natural, and that it is within his capabilities to adapt to it. Such a discussion with your child can be very important—primarily so that he doesn't feel caught in the middle and alone.

SINGLE PARENTS

Although there are more and more men participating in joint custody arrangements with their ex-wives, the overwhelming majority of single parents in this country are women. Many suffer a substantial drop in their standard of living, have to find full-time employment, and also have to cope with their own emotional stress following the divorce as well as the stresses and strains on their children. The period following a divorce can be a very trying time for a child. Feelings of anger and abandonment as well as anxiety about the future can cause a child to overreact or misbehave or be generally moody and out of sorts. Knowing how to handle a child in such a situation can be difficult. As a single parent, you may be feeling quite burdened—especially if you have more than one child.

Many single parents say that they feel they have to be both a mother and a father to the child. This is impossible, so you may as well rule out that idea. You are who you are. The limitations of your situation prevail. Many intangible attributes related to gender come into play when disciplining children. Males and females have different physical charac-

teristics, such as strength and tone of voice, that may contribute to differences in discipline techniques, and they also bring different
experiences to bear. A father disciplining a son, for example, has his
own experiences as a boy to draw upon, either consciously or unconsciously. As a single parent, you cannot be both a man and a woman.
Who you are is a parent. In order to discipline your child properly, you
have to draw from your own intelligence, judgment, past experience,
personal motivations and attitudes.

One of the stresses of being a single parent is that you don't have
anyone off whom to bounce ideas. There's no one to tell you if you are
doing the right thing, no system of checks and balances built into your
family. Without a spouse, it's difficult to get another perspective. This
might lead you to abuse your power because you have absolute authority. Or it may lead to negligence on your part because you have no one
to suggest that you might not be fulfilling your job.

To alleviate this potential problem, I suggest that you make contact
with any friends who might be in similar situations. Discuss child rearing and discipline with them, and see if their situations are analogous to
yours and if they can offer you good advice. At the very least, try out
some of your ideas and express your thoughts on the matter to them,
and see if they can offer another perspective. If you have any friends of
the opposite sex, either single or married, engage them in discussions
about the discipline problems of your children and see what their points
of view are. You may find these other ideas very helpful.

In addition, you may want to give some thought to joining a single-
parent support group such as Parents Without Partners, which has
chapters nationwide. There are also many parent support groups spon-
sored by community and religious organizations.

Be alert to the guilt factor in being a single parent. Because you may
feel partially responsible for the breakup of your marriage, or because
you feel that your child is being deprived of the other parent, you may
lean too far in the direction of indulgence. Be aware, too, that children
caught in a maelstrom of their own feelings may manipulate these feelings of guilt and try to exploit the situation. "If my father were in charge,
I'm sure he'd let me do that," you may hear. "Well, he isn't at this time,
so we'll just have to make our own rules," you might reply. "I know that
you must miss him."

Be honest and straightforward about your situation. Tell your children
that you, too, feel stranded and angry at times, but that you are going to

maintain the family the best way you can. The main idea to convey is that you are all going to stick together. Remind them that you're in charge. If you can demonstrate strength and conviction, it will be reassuring to your children, even if they object.

The wrenching emotions that accompany a divorce can be too much for a child to handle alone. If you think that the pressure is becoming too great, I suggest family counseling to help all of you regain your equilibrium.

DISABLED PARENTS

Obviously, if a parent has a vision or hearing impairment or a physical disability, extra limitations, as well as additional responsibilities, may be placed on the child. These must be accepted as a given, and the situation should not be compared with that of families in which there is no disabled person. Although you will have to make every effort to provide the child with appropriate learning and social opportunities along the way, and you should try hard not to impose an overwhelming burden of responsibility on him, don't feel guilty because of your disability. A blind mother might say to her child, for example, "Yes, it is too bad that I can't see. Therefore, you can't go out and play in the yard until the baby-sitter gets here." You may feel bad about this, but try not to weigh yourself down with self-accusations. To the extent that you are able, get extra help to look after your child so that he can go places and run around the way any other child can.

Sometimes a child may become angry with a parent because of the disability. Once the child is old enough to understand that his parent is different from others, he may resent being denied certain opportunities that other children have. This anger may show up in areas that appear unrelated to the disability, and may cause certain discipline problems.

The disabled parent may have additional discipline problems because of physical limitations. If you can't run after your child, he may, for a time, manipulate that situation and tease you. If you can't see your child, he may try to exploit that situation as well. Be alert to these potential problems and enlist the aid of a spouse or a helper if difficulties should arise.

EXCEPTIONAL CHILDREN

Children are considered exceptional if they differ from some hypotheti-cal norm. They may be hyperactive, too tall, too bright or too verbal. Or they may have emotional disturbances or suffer from behavioral prob-lems. There are many kinds of children we think of as exceptional, and for them special discipline issues arise. We either expect too much of them, or we misunderstand the cause of their behavior. The matter is an important one, since exceptional children are particularly vulnerable to abuse by adults. Even very gifted and precocious children sometimes suffer from their exceptional abilities. An adult, perhaps a teacher, chal-lenged by a comment or question from such a child, may react, "You think you're so smart! Just you wait and see!"

Each specific exception carries with it particular patterns of behavior. As a parent, you must learn as much as you can about the abilities and limitations that go with your child's attributes. We know, for example, that gifted children can be very challenging, can engage in incessant questioning, and can have a sense of humor that is different from that of other children. These characteristics must be viewed as part of this child's nature and makeup, and dealt with as a given. No parent should expect the child to stop being who she is.

This holds true for children whose exceptional behavior is not seen in such a positive light. Children with impulse-control problems, for ex-ample, are often clumsy and awkward and may slam doors, spill bever-ages, smudge homework and tear or crumple papers they are working on. To punish such a child for this kind of behavior is counterproductive and may cause additional problems rather than solve them. Instead, the parent of such a child will have to modify his world by using unbreak-able dishes in the house, by finding alternative ways to adjust doors and by making special allowances for the child's behavior.

A parent needs to learn as much as he can about what standards to impose on his child and what he can expect in terms of the child's growth and development. This can be derived from consultations with the child's teachers, from talks with parents of other children who have similar attributes, from specialists in the field, from knowledge gleaned by educating yourself in the matter and from your own intuition.

STEPPARENTS

Blended families, in which one or more parents is a stepparent, must grapple with unique and difficult discipline issues. Even the most sensitive and well-meaning stepparent is bound to feel confused or perhaps afraid of stepping on someone's toes.

First, be aware that a child may resent a new "Mom" or "Dad" because she may feel that this new man or woman took her own parent away from her. Even though this may not be the case at all, when children are hurt by divorce, their thinking isn't always terribly rational. A new spouse is a convenient scapegoat for a child's pain, and therefore may get more than his share of a child's resentment.

This is particularly true if your child is on the verge of adolescence. This is an age when even the best of parent-child relationships is strained, as the child is feeling both dependent upon and independent of the family and is trying to learn, albeit awkwardly, how to break away from this most important unit. She will have opinions of her own, and she will resent being treated like a child. She will bristle at taking orders. She will doubly resent the intrusion of yet a *third* parent at this stage.

If tensions characterize your blended family, begin by trying to ease up on any pressure you or your new spouse may be putting on the child. Then as a family engage both the new spouse and the child in discussions about the matter. (Or if *you* are the new spouse, take on this responsibility yourself.) You may discover to your surprise that each of you has many confused feelings about the new relationship that you perhaps take for granted. Let everyone air his or her grievances and feelings. If you think the relationships can withstand such a hearing, let the various parties do it in front of each other—without letting the conversation degenerate into a row.

A new stepparent cannot assume that she has an automatic right to a child's loyalty simply because she married the child's parent. This is a separate relationship, one in its own right, and will need time to develop. For this reason, I do not think it wise or practical for the stepparent to be a disciplinarian.

At the same time, a child must be given time to sort out her feelings about the new people and loyalties within the family. Be understanding and do not react defensively to what the child has to say. If the other biological parent is available to her, clue him or her in on the problem. Perhaps the other parent will be able to help in some way.

Your goal should be tolerance and mutual respect within the family unit. If conflicts persist, however, do not hesitate to seek the assistance of a family counselor, who may be able to help you redefine your roles.

AFTERWORD

I find it incredible that in 1988 there are still states that permit corporal punishment in the schools. And in many cases, this corporal punishment is not limited to a mere slap on the hand. Oftentimes children are allowed to be caned with wooden paddles. Not only have such measures proved an ineffective deterrent but, in my thinking, punishment of this sort is clearly abusive.

When one brutalizes children, one lowers their self-esteem, teaching them poor self-control, leading them into unsatisfying relationships with others and, in some cases, causing them to grow up to be brutalizing adults. While, as a parent, it may seem momentarily easier to yell and to hit, in the long run, abusive punishment and psychological maltreatment make life much more difficult for everyone. I hope this book will serve as a gentle reminder that a thoughtful, patient, intelligent and empathic approach will yield better long-term results for both you and your child.

INDEX

ABOUT THE AUTHOR

Dr. Lawrence Balter is Professor of Educational Psychology at New York University and director of NYU's WARMLINE, a telephone counseling service for parents. He is a practicing psychologist and psychoanalyst in New York City, and has been honored by the National Media Awards Committee of the American Psychological Association for his television series, "Children and All That Jazz."

Dr. Balter hosts a nationally syndicated ABC "Talkradio" program. His articles have appeared in numerous scientific journals as well as in such popular magazines as *The Ladies' Home Journal* and *Parents*.

Anita Shreve is a prolific writer on child care and parenting. Her articles have appeared in magazines such as *Redbook* and *The New York Times Magazine*. She is also the author of two books: *Remaking Motherhood* and *Working Woman: A Guide to Fitness and Health*.